VN

W. A. BROGDEN, EDITOR

W. A. Brogden, editor

The Neo-Classical Town
Scottish Contributions to Urban Design Since 1750

The Rutland Press, Edinburgh

First published 1996 by The Rutland Press, Edinburgh

© The Authors and The Rutland Press 1996

ISBN 1 873 190395

Designed and typeset in Helvetica by
H. U. Grabowski, London

Printed by Henry Ling Ltd., Dorset Press, Dorchester

Frontispiece: St. Nicholas Place, Union Street and
the Castlegate, Aberdeen, by W. F. Watt

Preface

This book grew out of a conference in late 1994 to celebrate the bicentennial of Union Street .

In 1794 the Baillies and Burgesses of the City of Aberdeen commissioned Charles Abercrombie to view the town and to recommend improvements, specifically as to how to overcome its land-locked, tight, overcrowded irregular nature – to give it easier access to its hinterland, to give it a suitable entry, and to give it scope for growth. In the recognition of these problems and in the commission to Abercrombie Aberdeen was following a lead established in Edinburgh in 1766 in the laying out of the first of the new towns; indeed, it was building on its own efforts from the same year – the building of Marischal Street to link market place and harbour. Similar developments had occurred in Glasgow, and seemingly innumerable new villages and towns had been established by improving landowners especially in the north-east from as early as 1715.

200 years later the Architectural Heritage Society of Scotland chose the phenomenon of 18th-century urban design as the subject for its annual conference – for many years now an examination by knowledgeable scholars and architects of subjects impinging on the aims of the Society – the study and protection of Scottish architecture, in its wildest sense, to include interior design on the one hand, to garden and landscape design on the other. The Robert Gordon University in Aberdeen was happy to join with the AHSS in organising the day of presentations. To this end there were lectures, poster presentations, exhibitions and workshops which promoted lively debate. The university had two purposes in this: to celebrate Aberdeen's achievement in transforming itself and thus to acknowledge the long standing close and happy relationship between the city and the university, and to acknowledge a similarly close relationship with the AHSS – particularly its North-East group, which has, since 1971, made a bridge between the Scott Sutherland School of Architecture and a wider community interested also in the study and protection of Scottish architecture.

From nine o'clock on the Saturday morning when the lectures began until well after ten in the evening when the Town Sergeant closed the splendid reception in the Town and County Hall in the Castlegate, town and gown listened, discussed and debated the rich heritage of urban design in Scotland from the mid-18th-century onwards.

From early on in the planning of the conference it was felt that the 18th-century achievements in the field of town planning could still bear reference at the end of the 20th century.

It is the exploration of this hypothesis that is this book's subject. The chapters have grown from the day's discussions, and have benefited from them, and the resonance of similar themes addressed from varying points of view. We hope the results can bear longer and detailed scrutiny. Certainly there is much new information here and new argument presented for the first time in print.

It is a pleasure to acknowledge our grateful thanks to Dr. D.A. Kennedy, Principal and Vice Chancellor of the University, and to Dr. James Wyness, Lord Provost of Aberdeen, who both officiated at the conference. For the smooth organisation of the event we thank Meg Thain, Thelma Blance and Neil Lamb. For his constant encouragement and support we are most grateful to Professor R. G. M. Webster.

CONTENTS

Introduction:
The Neo-Classical Town in Scotland
W. A. Brogden

The middle of the 18th century is significant for Scotland as it saw the beginnings of the remaking and phenomenal expansion not only of its major towns but also the smaller burghs and what seems at first glance innumerable villages.

The middle of the 18th century was also significant for European culture in which Scotland played an important role. Acknowledged to be the beginning of our modern era there was, among younger artists, an earnest search for a new and purer style of art, a style that would be at once impersonal clear and expressive of universal truths. They focused their concerns on Rome where they found ruins and fragments but they took delight in that. For equally attractive to them was the contrast between the pure and the elemental and its rough natural setting or poetic evocation in its ruined state.

These impulses, searches and attitudes are known collectively as Neo-Classicism.

In Scotland topography, nature and history as well, coincides with a period of enlightenment – of general education, sufficient wealth and optimism. Not only do the artists returning from Italy such as Robert Adam contribute to the development of urban Scotland, so also do the enlightened landowners of the countryside or the enlightened lawyers of the towns. The essays in this book address aspects of this development in an attempt to understand its history and to determine how much has survived into the nineteenth century and how much is relevant now.

The arts of the middle of the 18th century begin to manifest themselves in new places, and are put to new purposes. With direct enrichment from the experience of visiting Rome or Paestum, a resident of Dumfriesshire, for example, ceases to be provincial, especially as arts become increasingly a means to create wealth in the country rather than providing a filter through which a courtly taste is expressed. Even for those who stayed at home there was a sufficient

Previous page: Fig. 1 *Plan for Aberdeen showing the proposed new streets*. Charles Abercrombie, c. 1794, Aberdeen City Libraries

knowledge of the basics, for example architecture which, when united to orderly thought and recourse to first principles, would allow a successful attempt at design.

In the 1740s David Hume had encouraged the view that a more general disposition of luxuries would be beneficial to the country as a whole, and that a balanced pursuit of self-interest was good for all. Within 20 years his Edinburgh neighbour Lord Kames presented his clear and universally understandable theory of taste, and through his *Elements of Criticism* these hitherto specialist matters were available to all.

The design of towns does not figure in Hume and Kames as such. However, the tone of their works, and of others, exhibiting an air of disinterested inquiry, and the transparency of their language and argument would have encouraged a view that infra-structural elements combining warehouse, street and civic splendour were to be as easily grasped by the town councillors of Edinburgh or Aberdeen, as they had been by Augustus when faced with the irregularity of republican Rome.

Projecting schemes of urban improvement by the chief magistrates was an honourable activity, the expense was worthwhile, the imagination and knowledge to affect such improvements were available, and an inclination for private individuals to share and invest in such enterprises also existed in mid-18th-century Scotland. Its economic, philosophical and historic relevance was underpinned and accepted by a literate population. In Edinburgh, in Glasgow and in Aberdeen such schemes for urban improvement are begun, and with them comes a new urban architecture.

The Act of Union of Parliaments of 1707 had established money and support for establishing fisheries and the encouragement of husbandry and agriculture and the improvement of rural economy, especially through the establishment of linen manufacture. This empowerment was taken up by a group known as improving landowners, familiarly the Society of Scotch Improvers. Under the leadership of James Hope of Rankeillor this large group exchanged the fruits of their own experiments in agriculture, typically means to drain land (the very basis of agriculture in Scotland), or the enrichment of land by a variety of dressings including curious techniques of burning clay. They also improved their estates by making orderly and regular fermtouns, or villages. As Pat Nuttgens shows this was especially characteristic of the North-East. At least as early as 1716 Sir Archibald Grant began to improve Monymusk in Aberdeenshire by building simple, very plain, but identical buildings symmetrically arranged to either side of the axis of the ancient church, to which he added, also on axis an enclosure for cattle. In due course that enclosure is lined by plain but robust cottages. Thus are established some basic principles of urban design. A monument takes centre place, and if it can be both ancient and religious so much the better because it gives spiritual and poetic significance. From that a regular and hierarchical disposition of even very simple elements makes the place. If monument does not exist it is not so terrible: one can be added later, or its place on axis can be closed by another termination, and in due course the very establishment of the axis, or street, is sufficient regularity and order to give intellectual pleasure.

The varieties of village design are explored by Pat Nuttgens, and the establishment of streets terminating on monumental buildings, such as Shawfield House in Glasgow, is explained by Frank Walker where he argues that this becomes characteristic of late 18th-century Glasgow. Terminating axes by monuments lies at the heart of garden and landscape design also, and this is especially so in the gardens and landscapes of Italy and France so admired by Scots from the 17th century onwards. As John Lowrey points out in Scotland from Sir William Bruce's work at Balcaskie in Fife the substitution of natural (but extraordinary) features is exploited in Scottish garden design. Therefore, in the perfecting of Edinburgh it is the powerful natural feature – whether on axis, or as the 18th century progresses more Picturesque – as much as the monument that gives point to the composition.

He also gives due weight to the role of landscape planning in the design by James Craig for the first New Town. Thus not only are there obvious debts to Lemercier's Ville de Richelieu, Lowrey also shows how Craig's basic design is also part of that spirit of improvement that found it difficult to draw a precise distinction between laying out land for agriculture, for garden or landscape, or for a new town.

Joining the community in supporting urban improvement at town and parliamentary level, or even agreeing to invest personal wealth in building anew is established in Scotland by the 1760s. The composition of streets into a greater architectural expression is proposed by architects such as Adam from the 1770s. These proposals, however, meet with a variable response. In Aberdeen the houses in the Marischal Street project are identical, at least those built in the 1760s north of Bannerman's Bridge, and there is the suggestion at the surviving north-east terminal block with its gable facing into Marischal Street of something like a pedimented pavilion, and a similar arrangement can be seen in the South Bridge scheme in Edinburgh. But for that project Adam had proposed a more orderly composition whose acceptance required the various builders to subscribe to the design idea of a variable, essentially hierarchical, disposition within the street, and that amount of enlightened self-interest was too much to expect. A similar notion was proposed in Aberdeen, probably in Union Street, and certainly in King Street, but it, too, failed: the principle of regular, 'identical' houses, sharing certain limiting features to do with material, disposition of windows, and nature of roof was acceptable, whereas manifest hierarchy was not.

The handsomest of regular and hierarchical urban design was worked out first in rural developments more directly under the control of one man, usually the landowner. At Aden, related to New Deer, in Aberdeenshire, for example, the steading is of village scale, and it is composed into a shallow crescent of cart houses, byres, and other accommodation regularly laid out with a three-storey tower at its centre, and that ornamented by two Palladian windows, and topped by the semicircles so loved by the Neo-Classicists. In these more controlled projects can be seen the finest working out of this urban architecture.

It is to that sort of work that the early 20th century looked when, as Gavin Stamp shows the Duchy of Cornwall took a pattern for its south London development more associated to these smart farm projects than to the rather plainer villages. It might have been argued that this was also the derivation of those short terraces and semi-detached blocks so characteristic of Arts and Crafts work at the turn of the 19th and 20th centuries, and which were employed in Scotland charmingly at New Scone, near Perth, and somewhat less charmingly in the bleaker suburban estates established near most towns and cities after the First World War.

Most of the New Town of Edinburgh is made up of similar, plain but not identical houses, and composition of the rows in streets is haphazard, and only in Charlotte Square does the handsome achievement of the palace-block occur. Working with design principles similar to those he had used for the South Bridge design Adam composed the north side of the square into that grand statement which sums up the Neo-Classical town for many. Its central block, Bute House, dominates, in the sense that it occupies the centre, and therefore carries the greatest architectural emphasis. That is balanced by the broad terminal pavilions with their stylish sphinxes under pyramid roofs. The houses in between are more neutral, and indeed their type could be seen elsewhere. Only when the landlord was in control and had sufficient confidence could the palace-block work. It was attempted, valiantly, in Aberdeen, and there were variations on it near Glasgow Green and the South Inch at Perth, but only in Edinburgh does it become the pattern for development.

Even there it takes a little while for it to be established. The Heriot's Trustees could have insisted that Heriot Row was composed more regularly: they did not, and even Abercromby Place seems flawed. But with Reid and Sibbald's second New Town, especially Drummond

Place and Great King Street, the palace-block comes into its own. The pavilion ends are treated as blocks of flats, as are some of the centres, whereas the houses linking them were, at least originally, intended for one family only.

William Playfair and James Gillespie Graham discovered the Picturesque potential of the palace-block. For probably topographical and customary reasons in Playfair's Royal Circus scheme (it lies on a very significant slope, and the main road to Stockbridge runs through it diagonally) the elements of the palace-block are pleasingly disturbed, and with a much greater amount of urban parkland than elsewhere in the New Towns there is a distinct but not disagreeable irregularity.

In the Moray Estate the balance is very much in favour of the architecture: although Moray Place has a sloping site and a seeming irregular outline it is very much an enclosed space despite its size, and Ainslie Place and Randolph Crescent are even more building dominant. But even so, as John Lowrey writes, it is the Moray Estate that allowed Gillespie Graham to give full play to his Picturesque principles. He exploits the steeply sloping and serpentine site above the Water of Leith by making the bank and river into a garden, with his tall, gaunt and irregular wall of building along the skyline as if he intended to recall the effect the Old Town of Edinburgh has when viewed from Princes Street. His breaking up of the inner façades – those facing into Moray Place itself – is also pleasingly irregular.

The Moray Estate provides an almost Wagnerian finish to the New Town. Opposite to it, on the other bank of the Water of Leith, a quite different essay in the Picturesque was planned , at once more backward looking in its Arcadian simplicity, and also extraordinarily prescient in that it provides the prototype for the 19th- and 20th-century suburb. Between Anne Street, itself a diminutive pair of palace-blocks, and the terrace of Comely Bank, individual houses standing in their own large wooded grounds were proposed. Somewhat regular near Comely Bank the pattern is predominantly curving, even meandering making a park-like suburb of drives rather than streets, in which the houses sited apparently haphazardly and in relation only to their own specific grounds would have had to provide all architectural emphasis. The Dean Villas herald a significant change in the design of cities, a change developed on the whole outwith Scotland – at Victoria Park, Manchester, at Riverside near Chicago, and at Wannsee near Berlin.

In Edinburgh Comely Bank became a series first of elongated palace-blocks, and then more generalised curving terraces such as Learmonth Terrace, a form of development echoed in Glasgow, but, from somewhat different impulses. As Peter Reed shows estates were laid out, often around a mansion house, with palace-blocks, individual houses, rows of tenements, and villas, and such developments were in competition with each other. These disparate somewhat fragmented developments are drawn into a more consistent whole by the infilling of tenements to house the increasing number of skilled workmen drawn to the city in the later 19th century. The ring of the subway draws the city together even further.

Scotland led the world in developing its cities, and by the beginning of the present century these had become quite different things from what had been the case in 1750. Problems had arisen, and these appeared to be a part of urbanization itself. Overcrowded and insanitary conditions, usually in the older parts of town, had begun to cause concern by the middle of the 19th century. Water supply and sewage disposal were both inadequate, and being identified as sources of disease. Diseases associated with proximity and undernourishment such as tuberculosis join poverty and crime. These conditions flourished in the Gorbals (part of the bright new Laurieston alluded to in Frank Walker's essay), or in the Old Town of Edinburgh, the source of the civility so lamented as lacking in the New Town by Charles McKean, and in the Gallowgate of Aberdeen.

To Hume, or to Kames, as to other members of the Scottish Enlightenment, solutions to problems based on the application of orderly thought were, potentially, within their grasp. As Scottish cities grew and gained complexity so the universal pattern of orderly thought became specialised. The later 19th century, and especially the 20th century, made very significant distinctions between science, art, and philosophy. Patrick Geddes, from a background of studying botany, proposed regarding the Old Town of Edinburgh as a complex organism, so his suggestions to alleviate its apparent problems have to do with the metaphor of healing a patient. James Matthews and his colleagues in Aberdeen took an attitude to the same problems which was much closer to that of the Viennese architect Sitte for whom the formal qualities of old towns held the key to understanding and planning. For them the city is a work of art, and artistic principles should guide development. To the medical men charged with overseeing public health a quite different class of solutions was obvious – clean up slums, provide pure water, and at every opportunity increase light and fresh air.

In this century health and fresh air, and consequently lower density, focused initially on notions associated with Ebenezer Howard and the Garden Cities movement, and latterly on the more seductive imagery of LeCorbusier, have preoccupied Scottish urban development. Miles Glendinning's examination of that is thoughtful and stimulating. The 20th-century improvers shared many of the characteristics which made their forefathers famous.

A generation is perhaps too short a time span for a just assessment to take place, but the revolution that was unable to stop completely the Motorway Box in Glasgow invigorated the New Glasgow Society and gave rise to a passionate reassessment of the urban architecture of that city. Buchanan's 'solution' to Edinburgh's traffic – seen as relatively benign at the time – was successfully resisted, so Queen Street and Charlotte Square remain intact. George Square and much of the south side of Edinburgh were lost, in spite of the vigorous protests of the Architectural Heritage Society of Scotland.

It is a fact universally acknowledged that the 1960s and '70s were bad for our cities. And yet those decades saw the work of highly trained town planners, many of whom were also architects. Brian Evans' review suggests that two related factors led us astray. Partly through ignorance, and partly through folly, Scottish cities were despised as dirty, old fashioned or crime ridden, and sometimes as all three together. In consequence they were not respected, and were little studied. These attitudes were not confined to Scotland, and the perception of cities as problems encouraged an exaggerated belief in the efficacy of a model of systematic problem solving – itself naturally derived from orderly thought, but now understood to be either inadequate, or wrong.

In order to ensure that the mistakes of the recent past are not repeated we must try to unite the optimistic pursuit of the rational which was so successful in the middle of the 18th century, with some of Patrick Geddes' sensible holism. Urban architecture is perhaps in a similar position to that of the medical arts and sciences some 150 years ago. The art of healing may remain largely inexplicable, as will perhaps the art of successful composition, but in terms of systematic learning we do have some serious catching up to do. Before proposing any development either in an historical city, or in the countryside, the first precondition must be knowledge of what has gone on before, insofar as possible why it has gone on as it has, to which must be added knowledge from observable fact and common sense. Once the history of the place is known, in the sense also of a patient's history, then a diagnosis might by proposed, and a delicate, reversible course of medication can begin. Unlike medical practice, however, the care and healing of towns has to be done in public: most of the decisions to be taken are properly social ones, and, therefore, means of exploring different solutions, and presenting them to a wide audience for discussion, and debate has to be found.

Right: Fig. 2 *Plan for Edinburgh and Leith exhibiting all the projected improvements.* Hugh Paton, ca. 1822, Collection W. A. Brogden

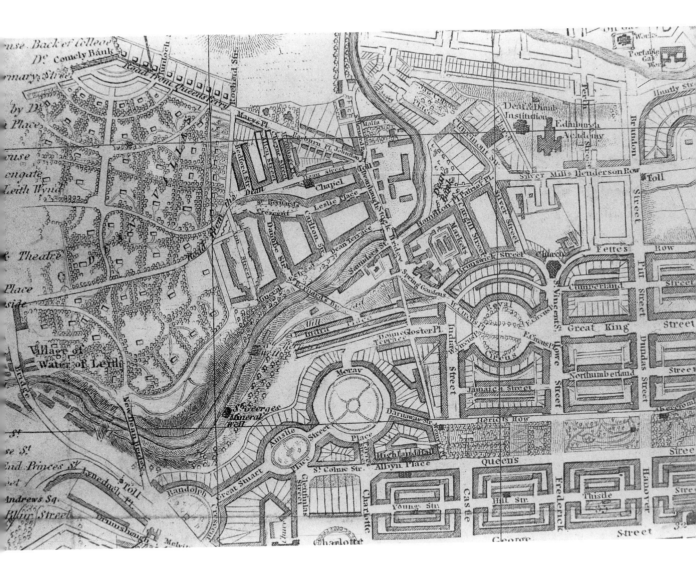

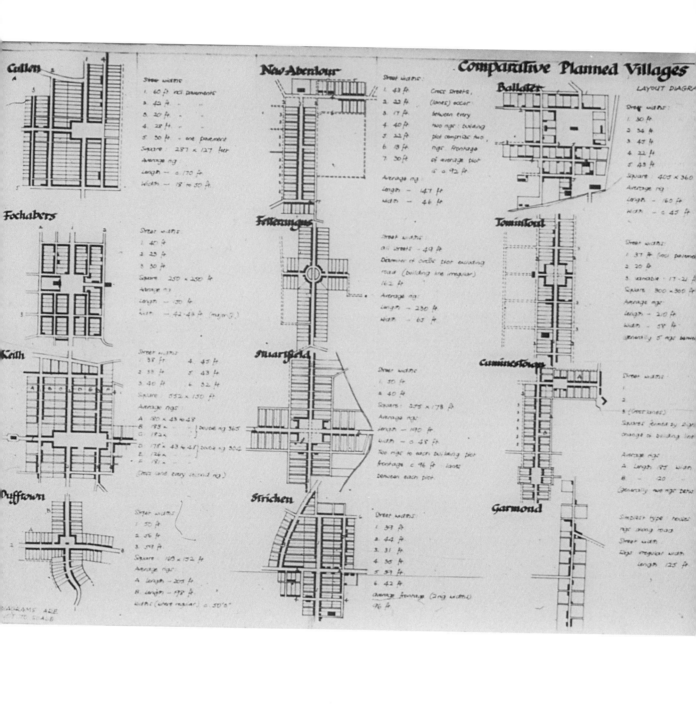

Comparative Planned Villages

LAYOUT DIAGRA

The Planned Villages of North-East Scotland
Patrick Nuttgens

Revised extract from *The Planning and Architecture of the Settlements of the North-East Lowlands of Scotland: a Regional Study*, a thesis submitted for the degree of Doctor of Philosophy at Edinburgh University, 1959.

The settlement pattern of the north-east Lowlands was profoundly altered in the 18th century by the erection of planned villages. Village planning was one of the major enterprises of the improving landlords, who created, almost from nothing, a whole village system (Fig. 2); and effected, without probably being aware of it, a piece of regional planning on a scale that is rivalled only by the burgh foundations of the early Middle Ages.

Fig. 2 *Map showing new planned villages and existing settlements in the north-east of Scotland. Drawing by P. Nuttgens*

The agricultural changes that transformed a series of farmtowns into neat, enlarged single farms and vastly increased the productivity of those farms, put large numbers of people out of their homes and their occupations. At the same time, the expansion of local industries and trade provided new employment. The years following 1745, when communications were improved and the management of land altered, were years of considerable economic and social development. The founding of villages was an essential part of this economic revolution. They not only took up the surplus population, but provided a means of stimulating industries to create additional employment. The movement was not confined to this region. It seems to have begun in the Lothians, where, as early as 1735, Cockburn of Ormiston was laying plans for his new village.

In this region the villages were mostly founded with a view to mixed occupations for the inhabitants. They were partly agricultural, either homes for labourers in the vicinity of the farms or smallholdings for people with another trade as well. In all cases the villages were designed so as to give a small plot of land to the tenant of each house, and a larger one beside the village (lotted lands) if he wished to take it and was approved of by the landlord. It was possible, therefore, for a villager to be either a hired labourer, a tradesman with the minimum of land, or a small crofter with a house and garden and one or several lots; and much of the subsequent development of the villages is the result of the fortunes of these alternatives. They were laid out by surveyors, some of whom were the direct employees of the landowner and some who were independent men paid for a particular job.

Previous page: Fig. 1 *Layout diagrams of some planned villages in the North-East of Scotland. Drawing by P. Nuttgens*

The peak period for the planning of villages was the second half of the 18th century. The drawing-up of the First Statistical Account in the 1770s provided an opportunity for comment upon them; and the editor, Sir John Sinclair, who had been one of their most enthusiastic protagonists, published in his *Analysis of the Statistical Account* (1825–6) a useful summary on the purpose of villages and the desiderata for their layout.

They were necessary, he considered, to combat the evils of scattered populations and of the towns, and could provide a useful centre for markets and for industry. The old Scotch villages he thought detestable; irregular and unpaved, they kept to the 'abominable practice of placing the dunghill before their doors'. Some people object to the villages on the grounds of their leading to the congregation there of the most worthless and dissipated members of society. But Sinclair found greater advantages. Villagers should be contented and unambitious, and have the pleasures of society exciting social affections and introducing urbanity among them. The villages fostered trades and gave the opportunity of a liberal education without infection from the bad company of towns. They improved the surrounding countryside by providing local markets and acting as a stimulus; they were an asylum for farmers and cottagers when driven from their possessions by the increasing size of the farms. Such people could become dealers of grain and meal, etc. Mechanics could go to the villages where they would be exempt from the restrictions of the incorporated trades in the burghs. There was room too for the day-labourers, a surgeon, baker, vintner, grocers, butchers, weavers, stockingmakers, masons, tailors, coopers, innkeepers, roadmakers, haberdashers, and even sometimes for milliners and mantuamakers.

Two small villages will serve as examples of the pioneer spirit. Sir Archibald Grant of Monymusk recast the old kirktown of *Monymusk*. Using the church as the key to the plan, he formed a neat square of houses and to it related the sites of his lint mill, bleachfields, etc. This is the simplest of all the planned villages. *Udny Green*, near Ellon, by Udny Castle, is another tiny village, planned around a triangular green. It seems likely that it was laid out when the fields by the castle were squared and when trees were planted along the avenues.

The procedure followed in the erection of a planned village can be seen more clearly in the case of *Tomintoul*, designed between 1775 and 1778 and begun in 1779 (Fig. 3). The site had certain natural advantages. It is a plateau about one mile by half a mile on a well-drained layer of old red sandstone. Furthermore a number of roads converged there. Adding to this the enthusiasm of the Duke of Gordon for resettling the Highlanders after the troubles of the earlier part of the century, the redistribution of the agricultural land and his keenness to foster a local weaving and linen industry, it is apparent that the conditions necessary to make a village were all there.

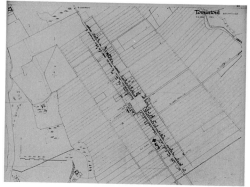

Fig. 3 *Tomintoul*. Drawing by P. Nuttgens

In 1770 the Duke took into employment Thomas Milne as his surveyor. He had previously been with Lord Fife for two years. In April 1777 Milne and the factor spent eight days marking out the tenements on the ground and the lines of the street (40ft. wide) and the square. The next stage, and really the most important, concerned the redistribution of the arable and grass lands surrounding the village.

Tomintoul was not wholly a success. Queen Victoria recorded in her diary for September 5, 1860, that it was 'the most tumble-down, poor-looking place I ever saw — a long street with three inns, miserable dirty-looking houses and people, and a sad look of wretchedness about it. Grant told me that it was the dirtiest, poorest village in the whole of the Highlands'.

Fochabers (Fig. 4) is an example of a planned village designed to replace an old burgh at a greater distance from the landowner's mansion: a conscious attempt to beautify an estate and improve the amenity of the castle. The Duke of Gordon simply demolished

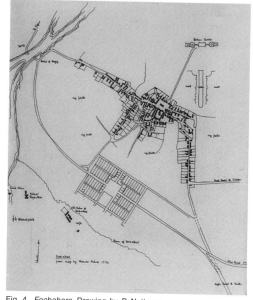

Fig. 4 *Fochabers*. Drawing by P. Nuttgens

an entire village and built a new one out of earshot. The village was not only further from Gordon Castle, thus allowing the Duke to develop its policies with a formal exercise in landscaping, it was also more directly on the post road from Cullen to Elgin, rebuilt in 1774, and conveniently placed in relation to the all-important crossing of the Spey. The new roads and the new bridge (1803) all formed part of an extensive scheme of replanning.

The plan of the village is typical of the slightly more elaborate villages, owing much to the kind of layout designed by Craig for Edinburgh. It consists of a main street and two parallel streets, with two back lanes separating them and acting as service lanes to the backs of the houses. The inn (Gordon Arms, Fig. 5) was one of the first steps taken by the Duke in erecting the village and was conspicuously placed at the nearest point to his new entrance gates. Most of the original houses remain. Some are harled and lime washed; all are simple, well-proportioned Georgian houses, and there are some excellent doorways. Particularly fascinating is the development of a real local character by the interpretation of the Georgian house in entirely local materials.

Fig. 5 *Gordon Arms Inn.* Photograph by P. Nuttgens

The planning of *Cullen* (Fig. 6) is an example of the same process of beautifying an estate, and it resulted in nearly as fine a village. The old royal burgh of Cullen, hard up against Cullen House, was removed between 1820 and 1830 by the Earl of Seafield, the heir of that Earl of Findlater who had been one of the pioneers in the agricultural revolution and had already been responsible for the planning of the New Keith in 1750. The plan was orientated so that one axis led to the gate to Cullen House and the other led to the sea.

The large number of other villages can be summarised more briefly. *New Keith* (Fig. 7) was the first planning venture by Lord Findlater and it was added to the east side of Old Keith, clustering about the Auld Brigg over the Isla. It was begun in 1750 or so and was intended for weavers who would also have a strip of land, and for

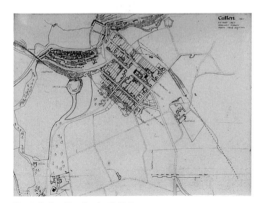

Fig. 6 *Cullen.* Drawing by P. Nuttgens

small holders who received portions of the 'lotted lands' to the east of the village. That it was successful is testified to by its later position as an important centre of the textile trade. The new bridge was built in 1770.

At about the same time (1750) the village of *Newmill* was founded about 1.5 miles away on the other side of the Isla. It too was a weavers' village, but did not prosper so much, and remains today much as it was laid out – two main streets crossing in a square, and back streets on each side with common cross lanes between every two houses. Closer at hand, and indeed just across the river from New Keith, is *Fife Keith*. This was on the Earl of Fife's land (hence its name) and he founded it in 1817 as a rival to the prospering neighbour.

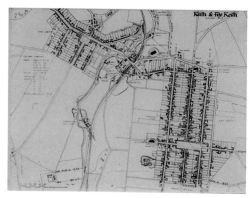

Fig. 7 *New Keith*. Drawing by P. Nuttgens

The junction at Fife Keith leads to Dufftown, and there the Earl of Fife (James Duff: hence another name) was busy in the same year (1817) laying out another village. *Dufftown* is a Highland village based on a rather crooked cross, with a square on one side of the main road very similar to the design for Fife Keith and presumably by the same hand. Dufftown prospered principally on its abundance of distilleries.

There is another group of planned villages in Moray. *Rothes* was an old castletown and untidy cluster of cottages at the lower end of the present Old Street. In 1766 the Earl of Findlater followed up his venture at Keith by recasting the village entirely, though on more modest lines than most of the others. *Archiestown* was built on the moor of Ballintorb, just west of the Spey, by Sir Archibald Grant of Monymusk and named after him. Established in 1760, it had the usual two main streets intersecting in a square, and back access lanes. It was intended to become a place of some importance, but suffered setbacks and remains today a small and rather untidy village. In 1783 a fire partly destroyed the village; and it was not until the 19th century that it began to be reconstructed.

Charlestown of Aberlour was begun in 1812 by Charles Grant of Wester Elchies. It was erected into a burgh of barony. As a result of the 'muckle spate' of 1829 that wrecked much of Rothes it took in population from outside. A long narrow street, it was mainly built up between 1830 and 1887.

Grantown-on-Spey was founded in 1765 as a centre for agricultural marketing and handicraft. The houses are nearly all built of a fine-grained light-coloured granite; many of them are additions made during the 19th century. Its main success has been as a holiday resort.

The village of *Urquhart* was planned at the end of the 18th century. From its layout, a single street with houses on each side and a T-junction at one end, Urquhart is a good example of a simple agricultural settlement.

Dallas, in the Highland part of Moray, was another example of an agricultural village and marketing centre. Its plan is similar to that of most of the other small planned villages. At Elgin itself, two important suburbs were built. *New Elgin* was built to the south of the old town. *Llanbryd*, belonging to the Earl of Fife, was entirely remodelled with uniform rows of cottages in 1854.

The district of Buchan witnesses the most concentrated establishment of new villages in the 18th century, nearly all of which were related to the agricultural improvements and to the founding of a local weaving industry. *New Pitsligo* was founded in 1787, entirely a new foundation on a site which had previously had only two or three farmhouses.

Strichen, originally known as Mormond Village, was begun by Lord Strichen in 1764. It was a much more successful and architecturally satisfactory foundation. The characteristic houses were planned for weavers, with an extra room for the loom. It was a deliberate attempt to attract 'tradesmen of all denominations, manufacturers and other industrious people'. *New Leeds*, not far away, was planned by Lord Strichen's son to be, as its name implies, a rival to its namesake in Yorkshire. The houses left there testify to its success. *Fetterangus* was founded by Ferguson of Pitfour about 1780. A simple village of two crossing streets, inhabited today by a large percentage of tinkers, its main feature is a roughly circular 'square' at the crossing of the streets.

Other villages in the vicinity include *Longside*, founded about 1800-10; *Mintlaw*, about the same time; *Maud*, about 1865; and *New Deer*, remodelled from an older settlement about 1805. A particularly good example from near the north coast of Buchan is *New Aberlour*, erected in 1798.

Another interesting group in Aberdeenshire is to the east of Turriff and was the work of one of the pioneers of the improvements, Cumine of Auchry. The first two were planned both as industrial and agricultural villages and as a tidying-up of the estate surrounding Auchry House. *Cuminestown* is a right-angle with one long side lying to the south of Auchry House; it was begun in 1763. A linen manufacture was established in the village.

Other examples in Aberdeenshire include *Rhynie* and *Lumsden* near the Cabrach. In Banffshire there is *Aberchirder*, commonly known as Foggieloan. *Cornhill* is an example of a planned layout on a very small scale at a road crossing. A type all to itself is *Ballater* on Deeside which was founded about 1770 entirely to accommodate visitors to the Pananich Mineral Wells. Enjoying a mild climate at an elevated position on a site of considerable natural beauty, it was one of the earliest spas in the north of Scotland.

The origins of most of the fisher villages are rather obscure. There are many references to fishing in medieval times and the burghs situated on the coast, such as Banff, Portsoy, Aberdeen, Fraserburgh, were involved in the industry. But the majority of the small villages seem to have been of later origin. At first the fishermen seem to have been crofters, and the older settlements often have cultivated plots. For, until the beginning of the 19th century, harbours in the fishing villages were the exception rather than the rule. The main period of expansion was in the 19th century when the herring fishing became a highly prosperous undertaking.

There seems to have been no lack of people ready to settle in villages in the 18th century, often moving east and south from Caithness and Sutherland; and the villages were placed within reach of the fishing grounds of the Moray Firth at convenient places for the shelter of boats.

The layout of fisher villages is quite varied. They do not divide neatly into unplanned examples and planned ones. Probably the majority are, in fact, planned villages, but they are not planned in the sense in which, say, Tomintoul was planned. There was no set street pattern or row of surveyor's houses; but the dividing of ground to make lots did give a regularity to the pattern of the village; whereas the inland planned villages are a layout essentially of streets, the fisher villages are a layout of houses or building plots.

Some of the best examples of the small and 'unplanned' fishing villages occur north of Peterhead and on both sides of Fraserburgh. Just across Fraserburgh Bay on the east are the joined villages of *Inverallochy* and *Cairnbulg*, and about a mile and a half to the south of them is the village of *St. Combs*. They are villages without harbours, the boats being drawn up to the shore in former times. Further west, near the border of Aberdeenshire and Banffshire, is *Pennan* on the estates of Auchmeddan. It is with one possible exception the most inaccessible fishertown in the region, huddling under the 200ft-high red sandstone conglomerate cliffs and quite invisible from inland.

Many of the fisher villages of the Banffshire coast are early 18th century settlements of the semi-planned type. They are all singularly Picturesque. To the east, sheltered in Gamrie Bay, are

Gardenstown and *Crovie*. Gardenstown was founded by Alexander of Troup in 1720, as part of the improvements he was carrying out on his estate. Crovie is supposed to have been settled at about the same time.

Cullen Seatown was certainly there in 1655, and was in much the same form as it is now at the time of the building of New Cullen in 1820. *Sandend*, a small and isolated village, is probably of early 18th-century date; by the middle of the 19th century it had some 300 inhabitants.

In all cases the harbours were built later than the first houses. Findochty was very small in 1766 and its nucleus was irregularly built around the bay. By 1873 its harbour had been made and more formal rows of houses (Siller Street and New Street) had been built to the east. Portknockie was developed earlier. Along the coast to the west is Hopeman, which was begun on entirely formal lines in 1805 by William Young of Burghead. It expanded in the middle of the century, when new harbours were built.

Specially notable was an exercise in planning carried out by the town council of Aberdeen at the mouth of the Dee. *Footdee* (or 'Futtie', as it is and should be called) was a fishing village, reputedly settled originally by Danes or Swedes in quite early times. About 1819 the Council determined to rebuild the village. The ground was levelled and 68 houses were built, forming two squares (North Square and South Square). A few years later, certainly after 1839, Pilot Square was added to accommodate the harbour pilots.

A remarkable feature of the villages which stretch along the Moray Firth coast from Portgordon to Portsoy is one curiously restricted to this area, though it occurs also further south, for example in Fife and in Irvine, Ayrshire. This is the vivid painting of the exteriors. It is difficult to discern any regular system in the choice of colours and techniques. Broadly, there are two types. One is where the stone walls are kept, but the joints repainted. The other is where the walls are rendered all over and paint is applied to the whole of the rendering. It may extend to the roof, which may be red, black, grey or even yellow. In the latter case there are normally three colours – one for the walls, one for the surrounds to the doors and windows and for the basecourse, and one for the woodwork.

The questions arise: when did this painting start and how did it come about. The general explanation is that it started with the painting of the boats in the prosperous days of the herring industry. While the quiet times were on, it was natural to paint the house too. It needed to be as watertight as the boat and here the paint was invaluable. There is also another factor involved. The painting was never done on lime harling but only on cement. It seems that the painting is a 20th-century tradition and an eminently functional one. But it has created some of the most distinctive characteristics of the North East.

Fig. 8 *Painted cottages, Cullen.* Photograph by P. Nuttgens

Grindlay's Close.

Crockei's Land.

The Incivility of Edinburgh's New Town
Charles McKean

The grandeur of Edinburgh's New Town, the magnificence of its Acropolis-like setting commanding the Forth Estuary, and the splendour of its public monuments gleaming in that unique clarity of Scottish light, seduces the imagination. It is as though it was always intended to be thus; and therefore implies the hand of a commanding genius with the power and cultivated taste to impose such order, graciousness and rationality upon these northern shores. It overwhelmingly appeals to our intellect, and is held to represent the world's finest example of classical town planning.

The truth is something different. The New Town was the result of muddle and pragmatism. It was never intended to function as a town, and its construction came close to killing its parent – Renaissance Edinburgh on its ridge – rather as though one of those birds that peck the backs of rhinos had penetrated too far. Indeed, the grandeur of the buildings has obscured what is perhaps the most distinguished feature of the New Town; and that is the fusion of two utterly different cultures: a Scottish Europeanism with that of England.

The construction of the New Town was a political act. The agenda is contained within the 1752 *Proposals*[1] made by Sir Gilbert Elliot of Minto to the Convention of Royal Burghs. The *Proposals* arose from an alarming condition survey of the fabric of the Old Town prompted by a disastrous tenement collapse opposite the Mercat Cross the previous year. The choice facing the council was either that of wholesale repair, clearance and rebuilding, or beginning again, new, elsewhere. In fact, the choice was possibly not as clear cut: it should have been a bit of both. Had Edinburgh been able to extend easily through simple growth, then it might have followed the pattern of Glasgow. The *Proposals*, however, favoured taking the opportunity of building on the land across the Nor' Loch which the Council had bought in 1717. It was a suspiciously Jacobite idea[2] which had become common currency during the previous seventy years. In these post-Culloden days, the ambitious Whigs now in charge, purified the idea of its traitorous taint and put it to work for their own agenda.

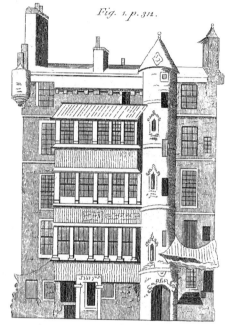

Fig. 1. p. 312.

The House at Edinburgh, where Mary Queen of Scots was confined.

Fig. 2 *The Black Turnpike, High Street*, Collection McKean

1. *Proposals for carrying on Certain Public Works in the City of Edinburgh*, Edinburgh 1752, reprint 1982.

2. *The Earl of Mar's Legacies to Scotland, and to his son Lord Erskine*, 1722–7, Scottish History Society, Vol. XXVI, Edinburgh 1896, pp. 201–3.

Previous page: Fig. 1 *Edinburgh, West Bow*. Copy of Elevation by Thomas Hamilton, Chrystal Collection, taken between 1900-30. The Royal Commisson on the Ancient and Historical Monuments of Scotland.

'Now that the rage of faction is abated' wrote Minto: now, in short, that the fifty years of Jacobite uncertainty was at an end, and Edinburgh could no longer aspire to being the capital of an independent country, the capital's purpose was to be redefined. It was destined to become the capital of North Britain; but if it was going to attract back its Scottish-sourced British aristocrats who had emigrated to London, it had to be made more attractive. For the aristos had rejected the hugger-mugger of Renaissance Edinburgh on its ridge, preferring the amenities of the new London suburbs – particularly the wide streets and squares of terraced houses in Mayfair. In both physical and psychological terms, therefore, Minto's plan was to redeem Edinburgh from being physically and politically suspect by the addition of a Mayfair-on-Forth. The 'King across the water' might be Jacobite: New Edinburgh across the water was to be distinctly Hanoverian. The clinching argument in the *Proposals* was that the construction of the New Town would revive the North British economy through promoting consumption.

The physical implications of this proposal are the critical ones. Minto was not rejecting old Edinburgh simply because it was in a state of physical decay. The truth was that it was too, too European. It was damned inconvenient, certainly, with only one access for wheeled vehicles – a decided disadvantage to a mid 18th-century mercantile town. But that was only part of the issue. Old Edinburgh was focused around an enormous market place – the High Street – said to be the second largest market place in Europe. This enormous space went unpunctuated from end to end, closed at the bottom by the Netherbow Gate and at the top by the Butter Tron. The only exits from it were the myriad closes or wynds that filtered downhill on either side. People lived vertically and communally. The same stair – as Minto noted with distaste – might embrace a cross-section of society from a lord to a tailor. He compared them to vertical streets. The average height of the buildings facing the High Street was six storeys, getting taller as they used the fall of the land on either side down the closes. Many of them – although some had been filled in – still remained sitting upon arcaded shops or commercial premises.

Fig. 3 *Mercat Cross and the High Street, Edinburgh, ca.1787*. Drawn by Francis Grose. Note St. Giles on the left with an arcaded tenement. Collection McKean

There was nothing unusual in this by European standards, as you can still see in towns as various as Salzburg or Chiavari. But it meant that life was lived in public: there was very little private space, and those few houses or developments which had managed to create private space – such as James Court, Riddle's Court or the Palace of Archbishop Beaton in Blackfriars Street – were at a premium. During eight months of the year, people lived at a density reaching up to 700 people per acre; and this was the mainspring of the Enlightenment, the inescapable meeting of people with people, and the possible cross-fertilisation deriving from the mixing of class with class, discipline with discipline. It had its downside: the physical nature of the city provided many bolt holes for the dispossessed, the underclass and the riotous; and that same physical nature of the city made it possible for them to surge up the closes, like sewage up a trap, occupy the High Street and imprison kings and threaten governments. As recently as 1736, the Edinburgh Mob had shown in the Porteous Riots that it was still capable of an awesome power. Yet there was nothing particularly unique to Edinburgh in this: it might be compared to a smaller version of Krakow, or a larger Urbino. To the Whigs, desperate to convert Scotland into North Britain, it was suspiciously foreign.

The Englishing of Edinburgh was to be achieved by the New Town across the Nor' Loch. First, it was not so much a new town as a suburb, explicitly restricted to persons of a certain rank or fortune. Professional classes and below were expected to remain behind in the High Street, along with all places of entertainment. Class consciousness was, therefore, embedded in the *Proposals* and was to become fossilised in the actual plan. Second, it was to be pre-eminently a suburb, no commerce, no double-sided shopping street, no market and – save churches – no public buildings. The assumption was that Edinburgh's heart would remain up by Parliament Square and that New Edinburgh was to be a grandiose aristocratic *banlieu*.

The 1767 competition brief for the new suburb was largely without specification, save that the promoters sought order and regularity,

Fig. 4 *Union Jack plan*, August 1766, possibly by James Craig

Fig. 5 *Rectified plan*, October 1766

Fig. 6 *Final plan*, 1786

These plans by the surveyor John Laurie for New Edinburgh may show the evolution of the final design of the New Town.

and the context was provided by the *Proposals'* fondness for the wide streets and squares of London. It is now uncertain whether the final plan was conceived by James Craig: or was the regularisation by John Adam or William Mylne upon Craig's probably original plan – which took the form of a Union Jack – an egregious idea intended to ingratiate himself with the Unionists. The triangulated blocks that would have resulted were contrary to the council's preference for order and regularity, and it was duly rectified. The building stances appear to be large, and we may assume that the intention was that they were to be filled by substantial terraced houses on the London model – houses which offered the novel facility of a suite of private reception rooms on the first floor. The inconvenient social mix of the Old Town, apparently so distasteful to Scottish nobility, was segregated into class-coded streets: the wealthiest in Charlotte Square, less grand in Queen Street, substantial suppliers in Young Street, tradesmen in Rose Street, and the underclasses in the lanes north and south. It was a first step in the long march of permitting Edinburgh natives the liberty of never having to meet anybody of a different social class if they did not wish to do so.

Compare Glasgow's First New Town (now called the Merchant City) developed from about 1780 by Robert Smith on partially developed lands and open fields. It consisted, for the most part, of three- or four-storey flatted dwellings above a ground floor of arcaded commercial premises: a revitalisation in the classic idiom of the normal form of Scottish Renaissance burghs. When Robert Adam came to design blocks in Ingram Street, Stirling's Square and George Square, he did so in the form of arcaded flatted buildings – in a startling contrast to his contemporary design for palace-fronted terraced houses in Edinburgh's Charlotte Square. In the Merchant City, its short streets were designed to focus axially upon public monuments. The result is an impressive, if not overwhelming, sense of containment which later destruction has failed to dispel. It is a containment reminiscent of what used to exist in the High Street of

Edinburgh. Only in Glasgow's second New Town – George Square west to the Blythswood Estate – did the Edinburgh model catch on – and, even then, not exactly. In the Craig plan only George Street was designed axially to focus on churches at either end; the two other principal streets, and the five cross streets were open-ended – although 19th-century developments provided axial vistas and terminations for Dundas Street and Hanover Street.

Noble and usually exotically foreign ancestors have been sought for the urban form of Edinburgh's new suburbs. However, the somewhat muddled generation of the plan we now know implies that we might be better looking more closely at home rather than to France or Greece. The New Town plan has considerable similarities with those new towns founded upon the barren wastes of north-east Scotland, many of which pre-date that of Edinburgh by a substantial amount. For the most part, they straddle an existing road which is transformed into the principal street (as the Long Gate becomes, more or less, George Street in Edinburgh). At some point – sometimes in the middle (Aberchirder); sometimes at the end (Fochabers and Keith) – the street debouches into a square which contains the church, the town house (Strichen) or market (Keith).[3] Towns of sufficient standing had parallel back streets of less important houses.

3. See particularly the RIAS/Landmark Trust Illustrated Architectural Guides to *Moray* (Charles McKean, Edinburgh 1989), and *Banff & Buchan* (Charles McKean, Edinburgh 1990).

Edinburgh's New Town is the most extensive and most formal variant on that plan, as would be appropriate for the capital; although Craig's original plan with its central square shared the spatial looseness of the north-east towns at its edges. The final version, with its squares at each end, has a noble sense of containment and axial geometry that the original lacked.[4]

4. The different uses of Laurie's plan are discussed in detail by Harris (see note above). The existence of the Union Jack plan was first noted by M. K. Meade *Plans of the New Town of Edinburgh*, in Architectural History, 14 (1971), pp. 40–52.

Until the arrival of romanticism – particularly Robert Louis Stevenson's belief that a city was ennobled if its residents could, from within the centre, look out and enjoy the countryside – the New Town plan was considered insufficiently contained for its windy site. Although splendid views were obtained from the wide streets

Fig. 7 *Robert Adam: Charlotte Square.* RCAHMS

Fig. 8 *Sir Walter Scott's House: 39-43 Castle Street.* RCAHMS

opening downhill north and south, there was much unframed and unsheltered space on a notoriously gusty hilltop. How much more sophisticated is the shelter of the Moray Estate. The buildings of the first New Town are barely sufficiently large to contain the space – save the tight scale of Hill, Young, Thistle and Rose Streets.

Nor was the urban form sufficiently strong to surmount fragmentation in the architectural treatment of individual houses. By the 1780s, the decorative fungus of ambitious plasterers was beginning to appear on the façades of the western extensions of George Street. That impelled the Lord Provost to commission Robert Adam in 1792 to restore regularity and grandeur to the houses through his palace frontages for Charlotte Square. Thus it is only in Charlotte Square that the true potential of grand-manner classical urbanism is realised to the degree that it could be. So it was the architecture and the building design, rather than the urban form, that worked the trick.

Mayfair-on-Forth might have been the agenda, but in characteristic fashion the Scots remodelled that idea to suit local aspirations. It was clear almost from the start that the London aristocrats were not going to return, and that the predominant occupiers of the New Town would be Scots of mixed, and frequently professional, classes. Thus it was that the native building form – the Scottish-European tenement – also crossed the Nor' Loch from the Old Town to possess the cross streets. We can assume that that was not the original intention from the fact that many of these tenements are disguised behind the façade of a double bow-fronted Georgian villa – the most sophisticated example being the pedimented and pilastered façade to Sir Walter Scott's tenement flat at 39 Castle Street. The identity and individuality of the cross-streets of the first New Town have been unjustifiably overlooked.

The fusion between these two cultures – the Scottish-European and the English – was achieved to the highest point of sophistication in the Moray Estate. As in the High Street there is a uniform height of building which gives a sense of strong, almost baroque, urban form of varying geometries; and excellent weather protection. It is about as far from a London suburb as you might conceive. The essential tenements have been absorbed into the urban form in a seamless manner: framing each street entrance and acting as bookends to the terraces of grandiose houses between. The Moray Estate represents the assimilation of new ideas within the Scottish culture and their metamorphosis into something native.

From the very beginning the intended exclusivity of the aristocratic suburb was doomed. The city's primary place of entertainment, the Theatre Royal, was begun in Shakespeare Square, more or less opposite the proposed Register House, in 1768. The Assembly Rooms followed in 1772, virtually killing off those in the High Street and George Square. Within a decade shops had arrived in Princes Street and they infected George Street not long afterwards. By the end of the century New Town residents had become reluctant to use the Old Town for either entertainment or necessaries. Indeed, nothing could stem the outflow of Society from the Old Town. It was as though canal banks had burst. According to Robert Chambers, the death of the Old Town could be dated to the last party held by Governor Fergusson of Pitfour in his *land* opposite the Luckenbooths in 1817. Planners may propose, but the people dispose. The *Proposals'* intention that the new suburb should not damage the life of the High Street was overwhelmed by market forces.

If it was no longer going to be just a suburb it therefore had to become a town. New aspirations emerged: ones that identified New Edinburgh as the Athens of the North. Statues appeared at focal points in the central boulevard of George Street (now with its bookshops and wine merchants) and civic monuments – principally to the arts or education – came to supply the grandeur. By the creation of the acropolis on Calton Hill, the galleries on the Mound, and by the addition of clubs, banks and professional institutions, they transformed the aristocratic suburb into an approximate metropolis.

Fig. 9 *James Gillespie Graham: Moray Place*. RCAHMS

Fig. 10 *Edinburgh Assembly Rooms and Music Hall*. RCAHMS

Fig. 11 *The Acropolis.* RCAHMS

For a more detailed analysis of Craig's plan and its context see K.Cruft and A. Fraser (eds), *James Craig 1744-1795.* Mercat Press, Edinburgh, 1995.

Below: Fig. 12 *James Craig's final plan for the New Town of Edinburgh.* RCAHMS

To the measure they succeeded; the Old Town became a ghetto of the underclass. Yet the plan of the New still remained insufficient to undertake all the functions of a town – no double-sided shopping street, nor a central gathering place. No place to riot in. The inefficient and unresolved duality between the Old and the New Towns of Edinburgh has always given it a lesser mercantile economy than more concentrated cities.

Yet it is a breathtaking physical achievement that still, after corruption by cars and commerce, can catch the breath. But whether it is a splendid example of civility depends upon your definition of civilisation. If you define civilisation along the lines of Lewis Mumford – namely the inescapable meeting of citizen with citizen, with social and economic interaction and integration – then you could only conclude that the New Town of Edinburgh must be one of the most handsome examples of built incivility in Europe.

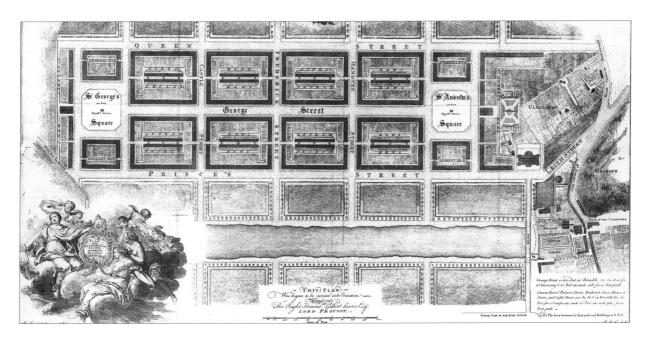

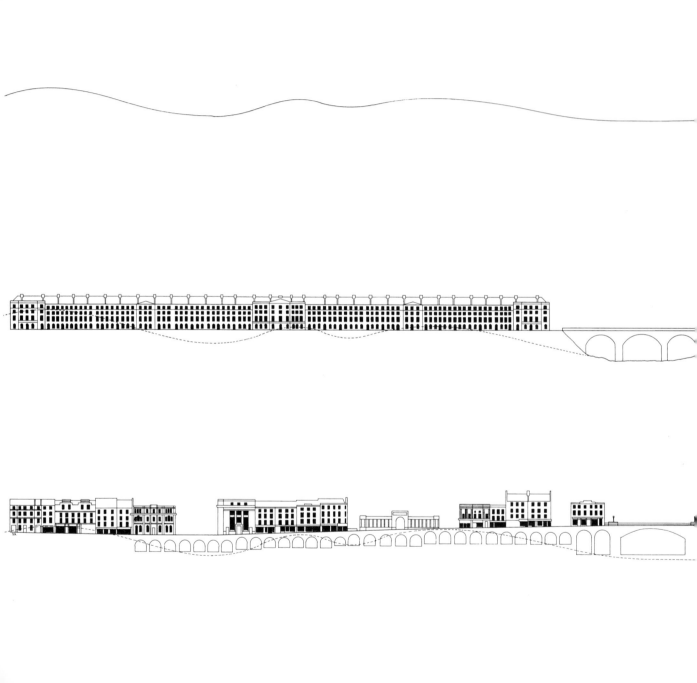

The Bridge/Street in Scottish Urban Planning
W. A. Brogden

The tight urban fabric of Scottish towns, coupled with dramatic sites and the laws of land tenure, caused Aberdeen and Edinburgh to become dense and overcrowded by the mid-18th century.

In both cities recourse to the bridge/street allowed leaps from the medieval cores to empty ground for development. These structures consisted of volumes of enclosed vaulted space and handsomely detailed bridges with buildings for various functions on either side. This new building type of unprecedented scale, and its mixture of public and private uses and funding, coincided with a highly developed stone architecture and the new aesthetics related to the association of ideas and the Picturesque.

The Bridge/Street

What is a bridge/street? Old London Bridge or the Ponte Vecchio naturally spring to mind with their superstructure of houses lining both sides of the roadway bridging the Thames and the Arno. That is not quite it; although the Rialto, and especially the derivatives by Scamozzi and others, gave both civic leaders and their designers the essential clues. In Bath Robert Adam made a modern and most elegant version of the old type for Pulteney Bridge (designed in 1768). In a similar vein were designs such as Paul Sandy's (later very active in Scottish projects) for a Bridge of Magnificence for London about 1780, typical of the 'projects' attempted by the young men from all over Europe while studying in Rome in the 1740s and 1750s.

Perhaps the curious design for a North Bridge in Edinburgh, apparently of the early 1750s and from the Adam firm, comes from these various, heretofore unfocused sources. The problem it addressed was, however, very specific and very Scottish.

In both Edinburgh and in Aberdeen decisions were taken to break out of the medieval town pattern by cutting streets through to empty ground. In both cases the ground fell away very steeply – on to

Previous page: *Union Street, Aberdeen, North-east section. Top, site section as surveyed by Cosmo Innes, middle, as designed by James Young, 1800, and bottom, as realised from 1811 to 1840.* Drawing by Andrew Younie

Fig. 2 *Marischal Street looking south to the harbour.* Photograph W. A. Brogden

Fig. 3 *Marischal Street and Virginia Street, before the demolition of Bannerman's Bridge.* Photograph W. A. Brogden

the valley and the Nor' Loch in Edinburgh, and from the Castlegate to the Shorelands and more significantly to the Denburn in Aberdeen.

In Edinburgh the North Bridge gave access to a new town whereas in Aberdeen the issues initially were somewhat different: the distance was shorter, the gap to be the bridged narrower and the object was to make a new street to the harbour rather than a Bridge to a new town. Therefore Marischal Street, as the project came to be called, presents the first example of a new type. Its street, or roadway, is carried on a series of stone arches, but only one of these is left open – and through it, James Law's Bannerman's Bridge of 1767 runs Virginia Street. The rest of the arches are closed. To either side of the roadway are houses of identical design – three storey, above roadway, five bay with granite ashlar fronts. To compensate for the difference between the level of the street and the slope of ground there are basement storeys.

An aspect of the crowded urbanity of Scottish towns is the tenement of flats. Already in the 17th century the whole house, or building is referred to as a tenement, a purpose-built series of 'flatted dwelling houses', that is one house per 'platte' or flat. The more flexible letting of rooms within an ordinary house continued in Aberdeen well into the 18th century, but in Marischal Street we see a series of flats – each of four or five rooms – served by a common stair and entered from the street by a passage between the shops. The passage and staircase became a sort of secondary street in themselves: indeed in Edinburgh they later became policed and lit by the corporation and are technically extensions of the street.

The disposition of Marischal Street gave it a civic significance – it connects the Regent Quay with the middle of the market place, which it addresses at right angles, and at that junction were two terminal buildings whose gables suggest pediments.

A similarly utilitarian bridge/street was begun in Edinburgh in 1775. The constituents of the South Bridge are identical to those in Aberdeen – vaulted roadway, open at the Cowgate only, lined by the tenements. These were rather wider in Edinburgh – up to seven bays – but the terminations were marked similarly by dressing the high gables as pediments.

In 1785 Robert Adam had been consulted in London about the South Bridge project by Lord Provost Hunter Blair. Although it is doubtful that that august client wished Adam to produce the improved designs he sent to Edinburgh, the marvellous scheme arrived and Adam did all in his power to see it realised. Adam made the proto-type bridge/street into architecture – not only highly decorated, but thoroughly conceived throughout: the Cowgate bridge becomes a triumphal arch surmounted by sphinxes; the roadway is lined by linked colonnade and arcade; the tenements are composed about slightly castellated centres with plainish wings terminating in fully dressed pavilions; the Tron Kirk end becomes a square while the college end has a crescent opposite its gates plus a big new hotel and assembly rooms – a fitting gateway to the capital of Scotland.

Adam was not the only architect to be disappointed in his designs: the infrastructure of Edinburgh – politicians, architects and builders – carried on with the project largely as originally conceived. At least Adam was to build the new University and Charlotte Square in the New Town, before his early death in 1792.

The late 18th century in Scotland was a time of great engineering projects – by Smeaton, Telford or MacAdam. In the North-East, as elsewhere, roads were being improved or created anew. In Aberdeenshire Charles Abercrombie was upgrading the roads from the Bridge of Dee and Bridge of Don into the town of Aberdeen. In relation to that he produced a *Report* (exactly two hundred years ago in November 1994) showing how town and country could be more advantageously linked.

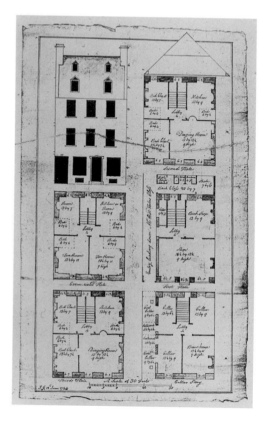

Fig. 4 *Aberdeen tenement, mid 19th century.* Drawing from Aberdeen City Art Galleries

The topography of Aberdeen made it extremely difficult to secure straight and level connections to its hinterland. The expedient chosen, doubtless taking confidence from Edinburgh's recent experience, was to cut through St. Katherine's Hill and create the biggest bridge/street thus far, which linked the market place with a great new bridge half a mile to the west and outside the town.

The design for the new street – called Union Street from 1801 – was put to competition. Sadly, only one of the designs survives, and that is not the winning one. It is by James Young, himself involved in the architectural infrastructure which ignored Adam's design for the South Bridge, but it owes much to Adam. Nearly half a mile in length it is composed of a pedimented centrepiece and two secondary centres, and terminates with pavilions. Its ground floor is arcaded (but not open). Young does not indicate the necessary secondary bridges or the vaults which would bring his proposed terrace up to the level of the Castlegate.

We must surmise what the winning scheme was like; it is very likely that it resembled Thomas Fletcher's design for King Street (as the northern arm of the project was called). In any event even that was abandoned, and abandoned very early. For the project to work it was necessary that the citizens of Aberdeen build – out of their own pockets – very large and very expensive houses, and there needed to be lots of them. The decision was taken in the first decade of the 19th century that the widths of houses could vary and that only material, regular disposition of windows, roof line and wall-head need be fixed. Adam had warned that repeating a standard design of house 'would certainly produce a very tiresome and bad effect'.

Was he right? Is it possible that the variation which comes from individuals following a similar pattern is actually essential?

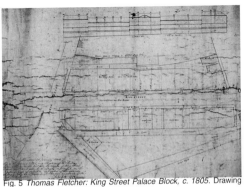

Fig. 5 *Thomas Fletcher: King Street Palace Block, c. 1805.* Drawing from Aberdeen City Archive

Swarbeck's engraving of the Bridges (as the South Bridge and North Bridge are known in Edinburgh) shows a very lively and interesting street in which three monuments stand out: everything else is subservient and, if not less important, certainly is in architectural contrast.

Union Street is similarly composed of monumental buildings punctuating a linear and strong but far from tidy streetscape. If there remains a design idea in Union Street it is likely to be that of the contrast between plain and fancy, and that contrast derives from the Palladian notion of centre, wing and pavilion. It is clear in Young's design; it is clear also in Fletcher's design. It is also apparent in William Burn's Bank of Scotland and Athenaeum at the very beginning of the 19th century, and it is equally apparent in Archibald Simpson's 40 Union Street, and at least until the 1930s. Therefore, it might be proposed that an unwritten, underlying but profound set of rules militates against the tidy, composed and elegant designs architects most love. Instead there may be an imperceptible rhythm of development with a very long memory.

Perhaps one speculates too much for an historian.

Studies of aesthetics interested philosophers in the Scottish universities throughout the 18th century, and Kames' *Elements of Criticism* of 1763, popularised these ideas and made the notion of association of ideas accessible to a wide audience. This sought to establish links between emotional response and, for example, architectural form. Initially it succeeded in giving a more intellectual basis for grounds laid out in the Picturesque taste. Robert Adam grew up as these ideas developed and in his last years he showed how topography and apparently old buildings, especially castles and fragments of Roman ones, might give colour and a more immediate emotional response. In one of his very late designs for the Calton Hill in Edinburgh he shows how 16th-century Scottish forms might be made into a bridge/street linking to the New Town.

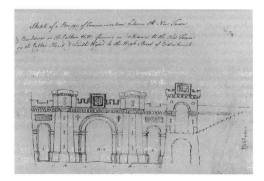

Fig. 6 *Robert Adam: Calton Hill viaduct, Edinburgh, 1791.* Drawing from the Soane Museum

A grimly castellated Bridewell occupied the plain west of Aberdeen from 1810, and a gothic design had been used in the 'centre' of a terrace in 1820, but the first significant built urban expression of revival comes with John (and William) Smith's Trinity Hall of 1846. Its colour and appeal to emotion is remarkable enough (it was particularly effective on young Victoria and Albert), but it also formed the south-western terminal pavilion to the Union Street terrace, and unblushingly regards its more classical fraternal twin opposite. By 1850 terminations were designed for both ends of Union Street in 16th-century form – for their Picturesque and emotional appeal.

Similar concerns occupied designers seeking to compose into some sensible order the great earthen mound in Edinburgh – a curious bridge/street conceived as early as 1787 – which became the dumping ground for waste earth from digging the cellars of the New Town. In the 1840s the artist Alexander Nasmyth proposed a sort of echo to Adam's Calton Hill bridge/street, whereas Thomas Hamilton suggested both a somewhat gothic and park-like mediation and, alternatively, after Playfair's Royal Scottish Academy was built, a freer rather Picturesque grouping of Greek Revival forms.

The last of the bridge/streets comes in 1888 and, although it is composed of the familiar constituents, it uses both scenic effect and an eclectic mixture of architectural styles. The tenements are grouped into blocks – each different from its neighbours – and these contrast with the monumental buildings – for universities, museums, theatre, library or church. Rosemount Viaduct has the utilitarian purposes of convenient connection between city centre and near suburb and of providing new and much-needed accommodation. It also obscured the squalid 17th-century industrial hovels in Gilcomston and replaced genuinely ancient buildings (such as the 16th century Jamieson's Lodging) with smart modern versions of them. At the Marischal College end – the 15th-century college – already largely rebuilt in the 1830s in a Tudor style, it finally lost its remaining ancient buildings in favour of the spiky Gothic frontage of 1896.

Fig. 7 *Union Bridge with terminal blocks to Union Street by Simpson (left) and the Smiths (right).* Photograph by G. W. Wilson

Rosemount Viaduct and Union Street form a sort of commentary on each other: the one shows how a medieval town can become modern enlightened, clean and healthy; the other how a modern city can make itself into an ideal version of its medieval self.

In the 20th-century bridge/streets have appeared as futuristic, even fantastical. When urbanity itself has been questioned – for the most understandable of motives, as sources of crime, civil and political strife, disease – and suburban ideas have become commonplace and enshrined in planning legislation, there has been little call for developments such as South Bridge or Rosemount Viaduct.

Scottish cities have, on the whole, not grown in the 20th century and where development or revision has taken place, it has been done on the principles of field composition – no lines, no terminations – hence no streets nor monumental stops. Does any town better exemplify the *Ville Radieuse* than Glasgow?

Yet the bridge/street idea remains with us. As a means of inhabiting either undeveloped, or poorly developed, areas near to strong or historic town centres it takes some beating. In Aberdeen it remains a viable design strategy even in the 1990s.

Since the 1940s there has been a recurring design idea – from an historian's point of view a very interesting one. Suppose the bridge/street notion is crossed with the field of pavilions format so common in 20th-century urbanism? Then it would be possible to span a great area in the heart of a town – hitherto a valley. The top will be a modern version of a park – mostly paved and useful – with parking, railway and roads below. That it precisely the proposition that Aberdeen is faced with and which it is currently debating.

Similar propositions have, in recent years, been considered in Edinburgh as well. Why not build over the Waverley Station and raise the level of the old Nor' Loch up to that of Princes Street? Why not, even better, extend that so that the two old bridge/streets

Fig. 8 *Union Terrace Gardens, Aberdeen. Proposal to form a bridge/ park with buildings by Ian Imlach, 1952.* Drawing from Scott Sutherland School of Architecture Archive

Fig. 9 *Upperkirkgate and the early 20th-century frontage to Marischal College.* Mezzotint, Collection N. A. Lamb

of North Bridge and the Mound become joined as a great green plain with a variety of pavilions, both old and new, ornamenting it. In Edinburgh initial reactions were hostile to lukewarm. The British Railways Board, or its successor, may find the notion much more attractive.

The bridge/street first appears in the Marischal Street project in Aberdeen in 1767 and, with Robert Adam's designs for Edinburgh in the 1780s, its Picturesque potential and enrichment from continental sources is further developed. The great scheme for Union Street in Aberdeen from 1794 transformed that town from its tight concentric medieval core to the rational Neo-Classical city it became. In Edinburgh, in the Mound project, and in Aberdeen in the Rosemount project the Picturesque became prominent and, in the latter case, addresses the same concerns as those which preoccupied Camillo Sitte. When combined with the park-like Le Corbusier inspired 'fields of pavilions', it presents a curious dilemma to late 20th-century architects and civic leaders, and perhaps a formal and conceptual vehicle for development in the next century.

The Emergence of the Grid: Later 18th-Century Urban Form in Glasgow

Frank Arneil Walker

Glasgow's 18th-century expansion as a 'planned' town is usually delineated in two post-1750 phases of urban development. The first of these is the so-called First New Town centred on George Square, the plan drawn up by the city's surveyor James Barry sometime in the late 1770s. The other is the Blythswood – or Second – New Town, that plotting of the 470 acre Blythswood Estate in an open grid-iron plan which was carried out in the last years of the century, perhaps by a 'Mr Craig, architect in Edinburgh...'.[1] This two-phase description is fair enough; it captures the essential major events of the city's expansion. But, in the context of a conference which is intent on making a close examination of Scottish contributions to urban development, it is inadequate. It is inadequate, I believe, on three counts.

In the first place, the description omits mention of certain key conditioning decisions made in regard to the city's urban design *prior* to 1750. Secondly, it oversimplifies the phasing of physical change and growth in the urban form of Glasgow before 1800. Moreover, although as I have acknowledged it describes the *essential* planning events, it does not offer any broader cultural understanding of these events; specifically, it does not attempt any interpretative relationship of spatial order and social order. In the very limited context of this brief essay I should like to try to make good these deficiencies.

Perhaps one of the most influential insertions into the fabric of 18th-century Glasgow was signalled with the appearance of the Shawfield Mansion built for 'one of the pioneers of the Virginia trade'.[2] Daniel Campbell, on the north side of Trongate between 1711 and 1712. The architectural importance of this commission has long been recognised. It is 20 years since Howard Colvin suggested it could be regarded as 'A Scottish Origin for English Palladianism'[3], anticipating the work of Burlington, Kent, Brettingham and others. Attractive as this thesis has been to us Scots (accustomed, until relatively recently, to find our architectural history consigned to the footnotes of English culture), it has perhaps overshadowed that

1. *Council Act Book*, Nov. 1791 – Oct. 1793, Vol.35, p. 173, Strathclyde Regional Archives C1.1.40.

2. J.R. Anderson, *Campbell of Shawfield*, in Old Glasgow Club Transactions 1919, Vol.3 (1913–18), Glasgow, p. 109.

3. H.M. Colvin, *A Scottish Origin for English Palladianism*, in Architectural History, Vol. 17, 1974.

Previous page: Fig. 1 *Shawfield by Colen Campbell, 1711-12*. By the 1760's known as Shawfield Mansion by which time it stood at the end of its street, Stockwellgait.

other, more *urban*, initiative in Campbell's action. For the choice of site was as deliberate and, in time, as influential as the choice of architectural style. The Shawfield Mansion stood at the north end of Stockwellgait, closing the long axis of that street in such a manner – in such a calculated manner – as to ensure that it would be seen by anyone entering the city across the bridge from the south.

Within a decade this *point-de-vue* strategy had been repeated at the north end of Candleriggs with the building of the North-West Church. In addition Candleriggs itself appears to have been somewhat straightened to emphasise the axial relationship, a relationship still further reinforced by the extension of the line of Candleriggs south across Trongate as the new King Street. Most importantly, since this laying down of King Street created in effect a right-angled intersection with Trongate, there emerged what a later 18th-century historian of the city would call the 'third and well formed Cross of Glasgow'.[4]

4. A. Brown, *History of Glasgow and of Paisley, Greenock and Port Glasgow*, Edinburgh, 1797, p. 82.

As a result of these events taking place before the end of the first quarter of the 18th-century, Glasgow's urban form already exhibited those three features which were to characterise its plan for the next hundred years or so. These features were:

1 – the planned right-angled intersection of streets, the consequence of which would be the emergence of the full-blown urban grid-iron;

2 – the evident concern that planned extensions of the city fabric should be geometrically (and, therefore, perceptually) integrated with the existing fabric;

3 – the addiction to *point-de-vue*, T-junction locations for important buildings – important, that is, in the sense of reflecting and projecting private power and public or civic significance.

Through the middle years of the century a number of streets appeared in a clear right-angled relationship with Trongate's westward prolongation as Argyle Street. Thus there evolved the so-called fishbone or 'double wooden comb'[5] plan. But it was not to be until the 1770s, when a second bridge was constructed across the Clyde, that, 'the public demand for building purposes being no longer restrainable'[6], major developments began. In a period of about 25 years, six distinct but interrelated phases of urban growth can be identified.

The first of these is the Barry plan of the late 1770s, the first New Town proper. This was the orthogonal layout which defined George Square. In it Barry introduced the grid, running north-south and east-west across the flat Ramshorn and Meadowflat Crofts; he co-ordinated this grid on the south with a number of existing streets running up from the Trongate and on the south-east with the *block* plan of an existing incle factory; and he ensured that street lines in the grid were tied axially to the façades of two merchants' mansion houses to create T-junction *points-de-vue*. What was achieved was a compromise between the wholly open grid and a more focused introverted layout.

Completion of the urban fabric between Barry's New Town and Glasgow Cross followed in the 1790s. This infill speculation at the heart of what is known today as the Merchant City produced more T-junction street relationships, for example at the ends of Hutcheson Street, Brunswick Street, Great Glassford Street (now Glassford Street), Garthland Street (now Garth Street) and Wilson Street. Some streets were also narrowed in order to increase the sense of 'gated' enclosures to the inner *grande place* of Wilson Street. The overall arrangement is orthogonal but the grid – if such it may be called here – is more closed and closing than open.

The third development to be noted is in Trades Town. This residential speculation by the Trades House and Incorporations of Glasgow, laid down in 1791 by their surveyor John Gardener, was the first cross-river suburb. But although separated from the main area of expansion in Meadowflat, its open-ended square-block grid

5. J. McUre, *A View of the City of Glasgow*, Glasgow, 1736, p. 133.

6. J. MacFarlane, *Hutchesons' Hospital*, in Old Glasgow Club Transactions, Vol. 3 (1913–18), Glasgow, 1919, pp. 200–5.

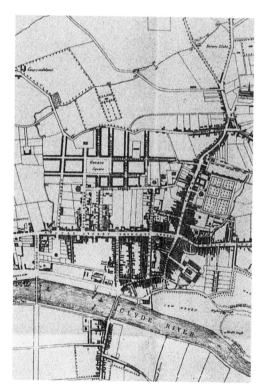

Fig. 2 *Glasgow, Barry Plan of 1782.* Strathclyde Regional Council

plan was similarly orientated and tied back into the city centre on the north-south connector of Jamaica Street bridge.

In 1794 the Hutcheson Patrons began to establish their own cross-river district of Hutcheson Town. Described as 'a regular plan ... laid out into a number of right-lined streets'[7], the development is an elongated rectangular-block grid. It is set out in parallel or right-angled relationship with the bend in the river and so lies at a 20-degree cant to the main city grid. This, however, seems to have afforded the possibility of axial integration with Saltmarket across the river – a putative link which occasioned the building of another bridge.

7. J. Denholm, *The History of the City of Glasgow and Suburbs*, Glasgow, 1804, p. 144.

A third cross-river suburb – Laurieston – may be included as a fifth phase of growth, though a date of about 1800 is as accurate as one may be. Like Wilson Street, it is infill; in this case extending the urban texture between Trades Town and Gorbals village. A measure of rectilinear integration with the Trades Town grid is maintained in a west-east direction while, like Hutcheson Town, a cross-river axis is proposed – this time the co-ordination of Portland Street and Abbotsford Place with St. Enoch's Church steeple and Buchanan Street beyond.

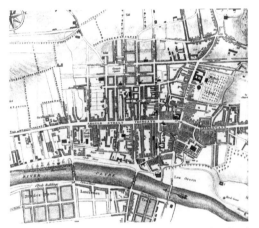

Fig. 3 *Glasgow, Plan of 1804.* In J. Denholm, The History of the City of Glasgow and Suburbs

Finally, there is the Blythswood New Town. In 1792, Colonel Campbell of Blythswood, well aware of the city's expansion on the east side of his estate and of the potential for profit this offered, was employing a 'Mr Craig, architect in Edinburgh ... to make a plan of his building ground in the neighbourhood of Meadowflat ...'.[8] What emerged was the Blythswood grid of the Second New Town. Whether designed by Craig or by William Kyle, the estate surveyor, this grid was well integrated with Barry's First New Town but, unlike the earlier Merchant City layout, it exhibited no closure whatsoever. The city's Second New Town, stretching across Blythswood Hill and Garnethill, was the open-ended Hippodamian grid *par excellence*.

8. *Council Act Book*, Nov. 1791 - Oct. 1793, Vol. 35, p. 173, Strathclyde Regional Archives C1.1.40.

Having quibbled with the superficiality of the description of Glasgow as a town of only two planned stages, I want now to re-assert the worth of that familiar view. To speak of Glasgow's 18th-century expansion in terms of *two* New Towns does have a convenient shorthand validity, for it highlights two general urban strategies at work in 18th-century urban design.

There is, first, the use of the orthogonal urban grid which is closed, contained or focused in some way, for example in Glasgow's First New Town (or Merchant City) by axial *point-de-vue* relationships set up between architecture and urban space.

Secondly, there is the application of an orthogonal urban grid which is open-ended, expansive and indifferent, a grid in which street-space is infinitely extensible. Here, whatever axiality may survive in architecture receives little or no acknowledgement in urban space.

Both these strategies exhibit gridding. To that extent both may be regarded as classicist. But only the first displays hierarchy. And in this respect, that is to say in terms of hierarchical urban space, we might draw a parallel between Glasgow's first New Town (or Merchant City) and Edinburgh's several New Towns – though, in Edinburgh, the concept of hierarchical urban space is much more fully elaborated. More usefully, however, I think we might make a deliberate distinction between Glasgow's *Second* New Town and the new towns of Edinburgh's expansion in the 18th and early 19th centuries. For, if Pevsner was right in his contention that our knowledge of the 'cultural geography of nations can only be successful – that is approach truth – if it is conducted in terms of polarities'[9], then we might do worse than acknowledge these two urban strategies as the poles of any scale of urban form used to evaluate the 'neo-classical town' in Scotland.

That such distinctions are necessary, that there was no clear-cut single formula, no universal model, applicable in 18th-century urban design is, I think, scarcely disputable. In his recent book on *The European City*, Leonardo Benevolo speaks about the 'debated

9. N. Pevsner, *The Englishness of English Art*, Harmondsworth, 1976, p. 24.

10. L. Benevolo, *The European City*, Oxford, 1993, p. 163.

programme'[10] of neo-classicism. He considers a plurality of approaches to have been possible and argues that whatever urban strategy was adopted it required a deeper justification than that adduced by mere taste.

How then do we read – or justify – these two urban strategies I have identified? How do we interpret their respective relationships of spatial and social order? Since the scope and length of this essay is necessarily limited, and since, with respect to Edinburgh, Colin McWilliam answered these questions 20 years ago[11], let me confine my attention to the Glasgow strategy, that is, to the Glasgow grid, that open-ended grid of the second New Town, which is to this day the most ubiquitous urban form in central Glasgow.

11. C. McWilliam, *Scottish Townscape*, London, 1975, p. 79.

Interpretation or 'justification', to use Benevolo's word, can be both practical and (again Benevolo's word) 'ideological'.[12] Practical justifications for the grid are its ease of geodesic application – with its regular equal measures the open grid is easy to plot; its ability to maximise the density of building plots – it treats the land in strictly functional and economical manner; its allowance for indeterminate incremental growth – to such an extent that it can ensure 'the appearance of a complete village, however small, and of a compact regular town, however enlarged'.[13] But each of these practical aspects of the grid has its equivalent, more ideological interpretation; interpretations nowhere more succinctly expressed than in Bernard Aspinwall's description of Glasgow as 'a democratic, mercantile and mobile city'.[14] The grid's regularity and repetitiveness, its equal measures, its absence of hierarchical space reflect a socially unpretentious, *democratic* – or at least quasi-democratic – community. The grid affords a simple and convenient pattern for acquisitive development; it packages the land neatly as a commodity to be bought and sold like any other in a predominantly *mercantile* society. The grid is dynamic in that its extensibility is limitless and its open-ended, regular, uninflected street geometry is experienced 'on the move'. In Edinburgh's new towns one is consistently *in* places and Places – Charlotte Square,

12. L. Benevolo, *op. cit.*, p. 163.

13. R. Rennie, quoted in J. Dunbar, *The Historic Architecture of Scotland*, London, 1966, p. 248.

14. B. Aspinwall, *Portable Utopia: Glasgow and the United States, 1820–1920*, Aberdeen, 1984, p. xv.

Moray Place, Ainslie Place, Randolph Crescent, the intersection of Melville Street and Walker Street, Coates Crescent and Atholl Crescent, Rutland Square, etc. In Glasgow's Second New Town one is constantly *mobile*, the grid affords little if any relief from the experience of going *to* or coming *from*. So Glasgow is a mobile city — both in its potential expansiveness and in its perceptual experience. It is a city always in some way 'on the move' and, indeed, 'on the make'. It does not stand still.

These practical and ideological qualities of the open grid do not make Glasgow a better city than Edinburgh. Indeed, it may be argued that the urban strategy applied in the capital — the use of bounded, introverted, urban grids, whether rectangular or polar; the creation of hierarchical, stratified urban space; and the close integration of architectural form with urban form (all of which are coupled, it must be said, with topographical good fortune) — has produced Scotland's most lasting lithic expression of 18th-century values. Edinburgh is *The Neo-Classical Town*. On the other hand, the very different qualities which characterise Glasgow, its 'democratic, mercantile and mobile' qualities, have made it, of all Scottish cities, by far the most capable of absorbing change. And this should not be surprising for it engrosses in its downtown plan an urban strategy the adaptative affinities of which stretch back to Miletus and forward to Milton Keynes.

Next page: Fig. 4 *Glasgow, Plan of 1808 by P. Fleming, Surveyor.*
Strathclyde Regional Council

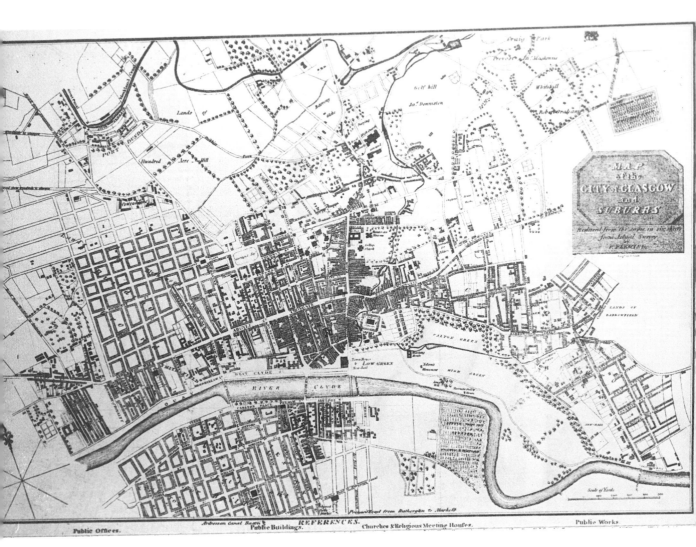

MAP
of the
CITY of GLASGOW
and
SUBURBS

Reduced from the large in two sheets
from Actual Survey
by J. PARKINS

Craig Park

Golf hill

River Clyde

Low Green

High Green

Glasgow Green

Lands of
Barrowfield

Port Dundas

Hundred Acre Hill

Scale of Yards

REFERENCES.

Public Offices.   Ardmean Canal Basin   Churches & Religious Meeting Houses   Public Works
                    Public Buildings.

Landscape Design and Edinburgh New Town
John Lowrey

The relationship between the New Town of Edinburgh and the surrounding landscape is an issue that has exercised historians and critics for a long time. The response to what is recognised as a spectacular setting by architects like Craig, Sibbald and Reid, Gillespie Graham and Playfair has been the subject of considerable debate almost since the first New Town was designed. Judgements, especially of Craig's grid, have on the whole reflected the attitude to nature of the time in which they were written. Eighteenth-century writers, most famously Stark and Cockburn, were severely critical of the lack of sympathy with the landscape and the lack of awareness of the principles of the Picturesque that they detected in the straight lines and grid layout of the earlier parts of the New Town.[1] More recent authors seem to have been influenced by these early opinions to a greater or lesser extent. Naismith is quite critical but finds a saving grace in a continuing connection with the Scottish tradition of burgh planning.[2] Youngson is also critical, arguing that the grid was already out of date by the 1760s and that Craig would have been well advised to look at recent and contemporary developments in Bath for inspiration. He concedes, however, that while the plan is mundane, its relationship to the site is very successful.[3] Finally, McWilliam's rather non-judgemental analysis of Craig's plan makes the important point that it is the informality of Bath rather than the formality of Edinburgh that is striking and unusual for its time.[4]

The general relationship between the New Town and its surrounding landscape is well understood[5]; however, it is possible to be rather more specific and to suggest that the New Town plan was not only related to the landscape in a general sense but was specifically influenced by ideas about landscape design. This paper sets out to explore that idea and will focus on James Craig's New Town plan, but will also go beyond that to consider the relationship between urban and landscape design in other areas of the New Town. In considering this matter, three main areas will be considered: the grid, the axis and the terrace. Having considered each of them fairly briefly, a final section will return to the idea of the axis and consider its relevance at further length.

1. The 18th-century view is expressed by H. Arnott in *The History of Edinburgh*, Edinburgh 1779; the19th-century criticism of Craig is contained in William Stark's *Report to the Right Honourable the Lord Provost, Magistrates and Council of the City of Edinburgh and the Governors of George Heriot's Hospital, on the Plans for laying out the grounds for buildings between Edinburgh and Leith*, Edinburgh, 1814; Lord Cockburn added to this criticism, for example in *Memorials of His Time*, Edinburgh 1856, 1945 edition, Robert Grant, Edinburgh, pp. 173-4. All of these are quoted in Peter Reed's important essay *Form and Context: a Study of Georgian Edinburgh*, in Thomas A Markus (ed.) *Order in Space and Society: Architectural Form and its Context in the Scottish Enlightenment*, Mainstream, Edinburgh, 1982, pp. 115-53.

2. Robert J. Naismith, *The Story of Scotland's Towns*, John Donald, Edinburgh, 1989, pp. 96–8.

3. A. J. Youngson, *The Making of Classical Edinburgh*, Edinburgh University Press 1966, paperback edition 1988, p. 79.

4. Colin McWilliam, *Scottish Townscape*, Collins, Glasgow, 1975, p. 80.

5. Naismith, Youngson and McWilliam, *ops. cit.*

Previous page: Fig. 1 *John Adair's survey of the Penicuik estate,1686.* Penicuik MSS, courtesy of Sir John Clerk of Penicuik

By the 1760s the idea that the design of a town could be influenced by the design of a garden was not new. For example John Evelyn's scheme for London in 1666 is a combination of a grid combined with two features taken from landscape design. The first of these was the *patte d'oie* and the second the *étoile*. Of more immediate concern for Craig's plan, however, was Laugier's *Essaie sur l'Architecture* of 1753.[6] Laugier was highly critical of the chaotic disorder of Paris and, in his suggestions for its improvement, drew a direct analogy between the city and the landscape, recommending that the lessons learned in the design of the latter should be used to regulate the layout of the former: 'One must look at the town as a forest. The streets of the one are the roads of the other; both must be cut through in the same way ... .'[7]

Laugier goes even further than this and argues that the landscape designs of André le Nôtre should be used as a basis for the design of towns: 'Let us carry out this idea and use the design of our parks as plans for our towns ... .'[8]

However, it is unlikely that Laugier would not have been impressed by Craig's plan for Edinburgh: 'There are towns with perfectly aligned streets, but since the plan was made by uninspired people, a boring accuracy and cold uniformity prevail ... everything is related to a large parallelogram transversed lengthwise and cross-wise by lines at right angles. Everywhere we have boring repetition of the same objects, and all quarters look so much alike that one is mistaken and gets lost ... . Above all, let us avoid excessive regularity and excessive symmetry ...'.[9]

In this criticism there is not only a clear indication that the Edinburgh grid is not what he had in mind for the landscape-influenced city, but also a striking similarity to William Stark's criticism of Edinburgh of some 60 years later.

However, this does not devalue the idea that landscape design may have influenced Edinburgh New Town. André le Nôtre did not form

6. Marc-Antoine Laugier, *Essai sur l'Architecture*, Paris, 1753. The first English translation was *An Essay on Architecture in which its true Principles are explained and invariable Rules proposed.* London, 1755 (translator unknown).

7. Laugier, *op. cit.*, translated by Wolfgang and Anni Hermann, Los Angeles, 1977, p. 128.

8. Laugier, *op. cit.*

9. Laugier, *op. cit.*, p. 129.

the context for the work of James Craig, rather a contemporary formal tradition introduced by Sir William Bruce in the 17th century, and lasting well into the 18th century, formed the immediate background to Craig's design. That tradition, although it was undoubtedly influenced by France, was also influenced by Dutch garden design and that tradition provides the precedent for Craig's grid. In the 17th century there were, broadly speaking, two approaches to the design of the formal garden. The first of these is represented by the vast parks of, for example, Fontainbleau which are cut up into hunting rides by avenues of trees that radiate from *étoiles* and *rond points*. The result is a design based on the star. The second approach is exemplified by Schoonheeten in the Netherlands. There, in a landscape which was hard-won from the marshlands, where the gridded topography derives from the never-ending battle against flooding from the North Sea, there was much greater interest in the productivity of the estate than in the pleasures of the chase. In Scotland there is more reliance on enclosures for agricultural improvement than for deletion or cutting for the chase: therefore, there is perhaps a superficially closer affinity to Dutch prototypes.[10]

To examine this idea and to assess its relevance to town design, it is first necessary to consider the Scottish formal garden as perfected by Bruce. His own garden at Kinross illustrates many of the essential principles of his approach to garden design and many of these are echoed in Craig's design for the New Town. First, although there is a fairly extensive design covering the policies of Kinross, there is a very clearly defined garden area (actually walled) which is the focus of the design. This large area contains the house and pleasure gardens and is rigorously controlled by a powerful axis of symmetry. This axis runs out beyond the gardens to terminate on Loch Leven Castle. The essence of this area of Kinross is a clearly defined, symmetrical and rectilinear area with a dominating axis that visually terminates on a specific building.

In essence, Craig's New Town design is very similar to this. At Kinross, the major move against the stately progression along the

10. This contrast, which is supposed to correspond to a 'British' (sic) interest in pleasure as opposed to a Dutch interest in economic returns as the guiding principle in landscape design in the late 17th century, is made in David Jacques and Arend Jan van der Horst *The Gardens of William and Mary*, Christopher Helm, London, 1988, p111.

major axis is by a single cross-axis, at right angles to the main one. This cross-axis leads us into the wider policies in which the dominant geometry is that of the grid, for the very good reason that it was part of the productive landscape containing enclosures for cattle, horses, etc. This adds to the overall perception of a landscape that is based on the grid.

Kinross was by no means unusual in this; most landscapes of this period, with the major exception of Alloa, are similar in their basics, if not their detail, to Kinross. Even large and medium-scale developments follow this broad pattern. Hamilton, although it has areas of great variety and elaboration, was essentially based on a single, dominant axis.[11] Penicuik was surveyed by John Adair in 1687 and the resulting layout is based on the axial approach and the grid.[12] Even in the 18th century this approach to landscape design continued to be influential. William Adam's designs retain something of the formality and the rectilinearity of earlier Scottish work.[13]

Smaller estates had much simpler layouts that usually consisted of an axial approach to the house and a series of enclosures around the house. Again, the axis and the grid struck the key notes in such estates. The main reason for this was that these estates were concerned much less with pleasure grounds than they were with improvement of agriculture. The impetus for that improvement, and specifically of enclosure, started in Scotland in the late 17th century and continued through the whole of the 18th.[14] The Lothians was a major centre for this spirit of improvement and Craig's New Town plan was related to this both conceptually and physically. Conceptually in the sense that the perceived need for improvement that had influenced the development of many of the estates in the area was also a major factor in the 1752 *Proposals* and the subsequent competition for the New Town. However, the improved estates were also important in that they provided the physical environment in which Craig's New Town was to be built. In this context one of the most interesting things about Laurie's 'New

11. Alexander Edward, who was Bruce's draughtsman at Kinross, designed Hamilton in 1708. The drawing is now in the possession of the Duke of Hamilton at Lennoxlove, East Lothian.

12. Scottish Record Office, RHP 9369, 9370 & 9371.

13. For example his design for Arniston.

14. Ian Whyte, *Agriculture and Society in Seventeenth-Century Scotland*, John Donald, Edinburgh 1979, Chapter 5: *The Country House and Enclosure*.

Edinburgh' plans of 1766 is not what they tell us about Craig's original intentions for the New Town, but rather that the environs of the city were composed of a whole series of enclosed pasture lands creating a grid-like landscape for Craig's grid-like town design.[15] That impression of the landscape around Edinburgh, and further afield, is borne out by other surveys, notably the one by William Roy carried out in the aftermath of the 1745 rebellion. It is even borne out by the one significant piece of large-scale landscape design specifically related to leisure that immediately preceded Craig's plan. The Meadows were laid out to the south of the city in 1738 by Mr Hope of Rankeillor and the design of the area is dominated by a rectilinear layout of parkland and walks and has a dominant vista linking back to the city (Fig. 2).

In this discussion of the grid it has also become clear that the grid was usually combined with a major avenue of approach: a dominant axis. The major axis in Craig's grid is, of course, George Street. It is wider than the other streets and it is terminated by buildings at each end. The terminating buildings, originally intended to be churches, are preceded by a square. So strong is the emphasis on this main axis that far from introducing anything that might undermine it at the squares (for example, a north-south axis through the centre of the squares), Craig, in his final manuscript plan of 1767, actually chose to enhance it. He did this by placing an obelisk in the centre of the square and then, to emphasise that it should be viewed along the George Street axis, he framed it with a pair of unspecified monuments that take up the axis of the main street and continue it across the open space of the square.

In execution the George Street axis was not built according to Craig's design, but what actually happened strengthens the relationship between the city plan and the landscape ideas that influenced it. Laurence Dundas acquired the church site in St. Andrew Square and commissioned Sir William Chambers to build him a house there in 1771.[16] The result was not a town house but a Palladian villa. Dundas and Chambers were well aware that by

15. The actual purpose of the Laurie plans was to indicate the quantity and the nature of the pasture lands around the city. I am grateful to Anthony Lewis for this information.

Fig. 2 'An Ancient Plan of the City of Edinburgh and its Environs' by Robert Kirkwood, 1817. Based on earlier surveys to show the city c.1750

16. John Harris, *Sir William Chambers: Knights of the Polar Star*, Zwemmer, London, 1970; pp. 71-2 & 207-8.

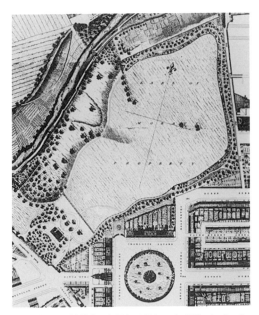

Fig. 3 *Survey of Edinburgh.* Robert Kirkwood, 1819, showing the Moray Estate just before it was laid out

17. John Harris, *op. cit.,* p. 70.

18. Alan Tait, *The Landscape Garden in Scotland 1735–1835,* Edinburgh University Press, 1980, p. 9.

19. The northern prospect of Frederick Street was closed by Playfair's St. Stephen's Church in 1827 and down Hanover Street was emphatically closed by a gasworks in the early 19th century.

20. This is a particularly sophisticated version of Bruce's use of objects and buildings outside the formal landscape being used to terminate an axis. He did this at Balcaskie, for example, where the Bass Rock terminates his main avenue. This became standard practice in the work of both Bruce and Alexander Edward in the late 17th and early 18th centuries at places like Kinnaird, Kinross and Hopetoun. It continued to be influential in the early 19th century; in the eastern New Town, for example, Bellevue Church terminates one end of the East Claremont Street axis. At the other end the street looks out over Powderhall and Bonnington. In the 1820s this was a relatively undeveloped, semi-industrial area (just like now) beyond which lay North Leith and the commanding spire of William Burn's North Leith Parish Church.

siting a house on the George Street axis, as the eastern culmination of the New Town, it gained the kind of prominence a country house would have in its own setting. George Street forms an urban avenue and the square becomes a kind of outer court. The house is set back from the street and thus creates a *cour d'honneur.* Beyond that is the house and behind that an informal garden, implausibly (though apparently accurately) likened to Kew.[17] In this way, the sequence of spaces leading up to, and through, Dundas House, can be likened to the country house and its designed landscape. More specifically, the point made above about the similarity between the New Town plan and the plan of Kinross bears repetition here. Tait's summary of the Bruce method of landscape design: '... a series of repetitive enclosures ... centred upon a broad axial vista ...', is almost equally applicable to Craig's New Town.[18]

Axial planning became the norm in most subsequent New Town development. Occasionally this involved an existing country house; in 1774, for example, Robert Adam built Bellevue House in what later became Drummond Place. This was the major eastern space of Reid and Sibbald's second New Town but in this case the house could not terminate the major axis of Great King Street and instead addressed the cross-axis of Dublin Street. The cross-axes of the rest of the New Town were also given major buildings to terminate them.[19] In one case this idea was developed into something more sophisticated. The southern view from George Street along Hanover Street is closed by the Royal Scottish Academy building. However, from the north side of the George Street ridge Playfair's building is invisible and the vista was closed first by Gillespie Graham and Pugin's Tolbooth Church (1839–44) which was then visually combined with Playfair's New College (1845–50) in a superb scenographic ensemble which closes the vista and formally related the Old and New Towns.[20]

While the focused view is a major characteristic of the New Town so, paradoxically, is the open or unfocused view. Indeed the one element in Craig's design that is widely acknowledged as a success is his use of one-sided streets on the north and south edges of his design. In this way a broad panorama is opened to the north, and a dramatic view of the Old Town is gained from the south (Fig. 4).[21]

This introduces the third element in our city/garden analogy: the terrace. These views, especially to the north, can be linked to the tradition of Scottish terraced gardens. Gardens like Hatton or Culross Palace enjoyed similar open views across the countryside. At the beginning of the 18th century, the Culross terraces were answered on the opposite bank of the Forth by the terrace walk at Hopetoun. Macky, in his *Tour*, was very excited by this, claiming it was the best he had ever seen and linking it with Italian gardens like Frascati and St Michael del Bosco (Bologna). A more immediate influence may have been the great terrace at St Germain that Alexander Edward certainly saw on his visit there in 1701.[22]

It is quite easy to interpret Queen Street in particular as a great formal terrace, overlooking the countryside towards Fife and beyond. However, there is another aspect of this juxtaposition of the formal and informal that echoes landscape design. Most authors have commented on the very effective contrast between Old and New Town and the way in which Craig's design allows this to be exploited; that element of contrast is also a feature of some 18th-century landscape design, notably William Adam's Chatelherault. There, Adam's hunting lodge terminates a grand, formal landscape but also introduces the wild landscape of the gorge, on the one hand, and towards a formal parterre behind the hunting lodge, on the other.[23] This is analogous to Craig's New Town design, with its sharp contrast between the formality of the new and the irregularity of the old. It was in that contrast that Robert Louis Stevenson later found the 'essence of the Picturesque' in Edinburgh.[24]

Finally, there is one area of the New Town that pulls much of this together. The Moray estate combines the formal and picturesque, the axial and the open view, and incorporates an existing country house into an urban design. The site, to the north-west of Charlotte

21. One author has gone so far as to dub Craig 'a city planning genius' (along with Wood the Younger), see A. E. J. Morris, *History of Urban Form Before the Industrial Revolution*, 3rd edition, Longmans, Harlow, 1994, p. 279, note 97.

22. John Lowrey, *A Man of Excellent Parts. Alexander Edward: Architect, Jacobite, Clergyman*, Crawford Centre for the Arts, University of St Andrews, 1987, p. 22.

23. John, Lowrey, *The Development of the Formal Landscape at Hamilton 1700–1750*, in Frew & Jones (eds.), *Aspects of Scottish Classicism: the House and its Formal Setting 1690–1750*, St Andrews Studies in the History of Scottish Architecture and Design, University of St Andrews 1988, p. 29. One point that is made here is that Adam's inspiration for the contrast of the two types of landscape may have been terraced gardens at Barncluith, only half a mile from Chatelherault.

24. The idea of contrast is important in understanding the way in which the city and landscape interact, in other words of the picturesque in Edinburgh. In an area like the Calton Hill, for example, Playfair's treatment of the hilltop is quite unlike John Wood's sequence of streets and terraces at Lansdown in Bath. Rather than sensitively following the contours of the site, Playfair achieves his effect partly by contrasting the severely formal palace frontage of Royal Terrace with the much more relaxed elevations of Regent Terrace.

square, was highly Picturesque. It overlooked the wooded valley of the Water of Leith and was close to St. Bernard's Well, a landscape building that nicely symbolises the relationship between city and landscape that is so important in Edinburgh.

The scenic value of the spot was most famously appreciated by Lord Cockburn:

"It was about this time that the Earl of Moray's ground to the north of Charlotte Square began to be broken up for building purposes. It was then an open field of as green turf as Scotland could boast of, with a few respectable trees on the flat, and thickly wooded on the bank along the Water of Leith. Moray Place and Ainslie Place stand there now. It was the beginning of a sad change, as we then felt. That well kept and almost evergreen field was the most beautiful piece of ground in immediate connection with the town, and led the eye agreeably over our distant northern scenery. How glorious the prospect, on a summer evening, from Queen Street! We had got into the habit of believing that the mere charm of the ground would keep it sacred, and were inclined to cling to our conviction even after we saw the foundations digging ... But how can I forget the glory of that scene ... I have stood in Queen Street, or the opening at the north-west corner of Charlotte Square, and listened to the ceaseless rural corn crakes, nestling happily in the dewy grass.'[26]

26. Cockburn, *op. cit.*, pp. 229–30.

This was clearly a site tailor-made for a designer schooled in the principles of the Picturesque, which by 1822, when James Gillespie Graham started work on this very high-class development, was pretty well established.

In fact, Gillespie Graham's houses appear to turn their backs on the superb views down to the Water of Leith and across to the countryside beyond. The layout is inward-looking and, at first glance, appears to be more concerned with formal geometry than picturesque variety. However, it would be a mistake to think of the

Moray estate as simply an introverted and formal design. There are two important considerations that appear to have been overlooked.[27] First, Gillespie Graham's design is required not only to take account of the landscape, but also of the existing country house belonging to the earl. When that is included, the design can be interpreted as a highly elaborate sequence of spaces that form the approach, the axis, to the house. In other words this is another example, albeit a highly elaborate one, of the focused, axial design. Second, the landscape *is* addressed by the architect. The gardens at the back of Moray Place and Ainslie Place formed a very important, complex and expensive part of the design. They are constructed on a steep slope with terrace walks and decorative iron railings that made these pleasure gardens unique in Edinburgh and provided an important selling point for the Earl of Moray, giving his development the edge over others, especially Calton Hill.

Moreover, while it is certainly true that the front of the houses faced away from the Water of Leith, the rooms at the back of the house were actually the most important ones. In houses in Moray Place, two out of three drawing rooms faced the back, as did the parlour and the main bedroom.[28]

This was possible because Gillespie Graham's concern with complex, but inward-looking, urban spaces resulted in plans that flared out at the back and provided space for expansive and outward-looking domestic planning. Finally, if this combination of expensive gardens and major rooms does not provide enough evidence that this was a development that did indeed take the landscape views seriously, the evidence that Gillespie Graham originally intended to provide designs for a unified façade on the back of the building, should be conclusive.[29]

27. For example by Peter Reed, *Op. Cit.*, p. 132.

28. I am grateful to Ian Gow for a copy of his, as yet unpublished, essay on *The Northern Athenian House*, which includes his reconstructions of the plans of houses in Moray Place.

29. David Walker, *The Donaldson's Hospital Competition and the Palace of Westminster*, in *Design and Practice in British Architecture: Studies in Architectural History Presented to Howard Colvin*; Architectural History, vol. 27: 1984, p. 489. Walker refers to Gillespie Graham's intention to build 'unified rear elevations' at Moray Place being thwarted by the interfering, but influential amateur, James Hope.

Next page: Fig. 4 *James Gillespie Graham, feuing plan for the Moray Estate, 1822.* Edinburgh City Libraries

I am grateful to Sir John Clerk of Penicuik, Bt, for permission to reproduce the Adair drawing; likewise to Edinburgh City Libraries for the Moray Estate feuing plan.

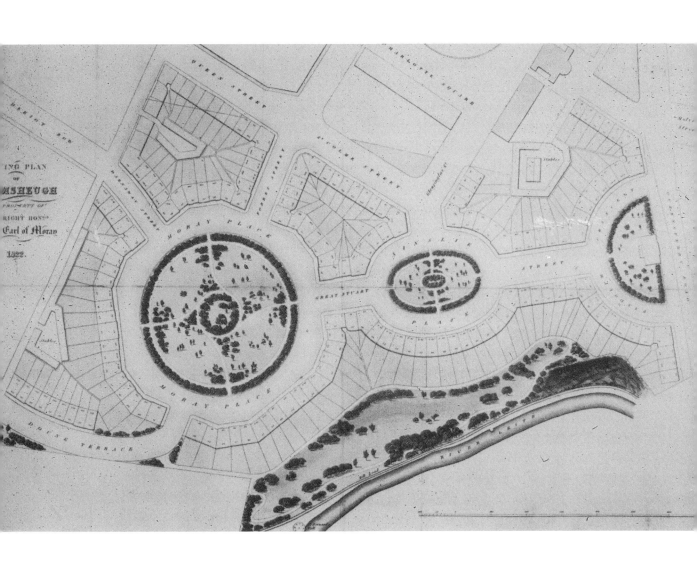

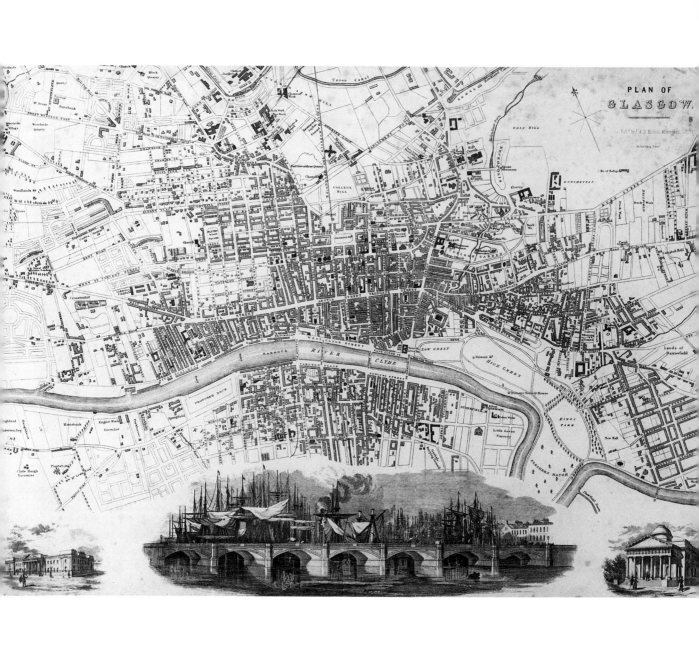

PLAN OF
GLASGOW.

The Breaking of the Grid: Glasgow's West End
Peter Reed

This paper draws upon Peter Reed (ed.), 1993, *Glasgow: The Forming of a City*, Edinburgh University Press, in particular, chapters 5 (*'The Victorian Suburb'*) and 7 (*'The Tenement City'*) by the author.

In this paper I take the Neo-Classical town to be one where a substantial part follows a plan, or plans, observing two integrated principles: the one, that the public space is geometrically organised in translational, reflective or rotational symmetries; the other, that these symmetries are articulated in the classical elevations of the buildings that define the public space. These principles – perhaps over-prescriptive for the purposes of this conference – are manifest, for example, in successive expansions of Edinburgh's New Town.

By this definition, Glasgow has never been a Neo-Classical city. Instead it adopted the grid. That is not to say that there were not neo-classical insertions into the medieval fabric of the city nor hesitant excursions on neo-classical lines from its edge. And, within the grid of Glasgow's first tentative New Town, laid down in the 1780s, were to be found the classical symmetries of George Square. But the wider growth of the city, to the south of the Clyde and on to the Blythswood lands to the west, was partitioned by unmodulated rectilinear grids.

No doubt reasons of land economy account for the early emergence of the grid and its later ubiquity in the expansion of the city. But there may be other, less obviously material, explanations. It is, I suggest, significant that Glasgow was never walled – at least for defensive purposes. For this meant that the middle classes, emigrating from the increasingly insalubrious historic core, could be accommodated in cautious, progressive additions to the urban fabric, rather than, of necessity, in discrete extramural settlements. And, of course, the open, extensible grid is ideally suited to this kind of marginal, indeterminate development.

As the map of 1841 shows, most of the population growth of Glasgow, in the years of its industrial awakening, was accommodated in incrementally expanding grids on the east, south and west sides of the city (Fig. 1). Not only were the grids freely extensible, they were open to any kind of architectural development.

Previous page: Fig. 1 *Plan of Glasgow in 1841*. Hill Collection, Royal Faculty of Procurators.

The Blythswood grid accommodated terraces, tenements and villas in no obviously co-ordinated way, though some terraces were elevated symmetrically and, in Garden (now Blythswood) Square, some were grouped around a pleasure garden. The map also shows that in 1841 there was much of the Blythswood grid not yet built upon. As it turned out, what was undeveloped then was largely to remain so – at least for residential purposes.

With the gathering pace of industrialisation, the gridded new towns north of the river were successively taken over by the commerce of the city, while the new towns to the south – Hutcheson Town, Laurieston and Tradeston – entered their long decline into infamous squalor. Those who, in increasing numbers, could afford to do so, began to look further afield for more secure and salubrious conditions in which to live and rear their families. There were, of course, others who sought to increase their own wealth by meeting this demand. All around the city, landowners looked to the development potential of their estates in what was becoming a highly competitive housing market.

In the many estate plans that were produced from the 1830s to the 1870s – and I must acknowledge here the exhaustive survey of the evidence carried out by my student, Tommy Tang for his forthcoming doctoral thesis[1] – we can discern two kinds of response to this burgeoning demand for segregated, respectable, owner-occupied housing.

One, where a site offered little topographical relief, was the adoption – for the first time in Glasgow, it might be said – of the neo-classical principles of geometrically ordered space bounded by classical elevations. The developer aimed to create a grand self-contained urbanity, with secluded pleasure gardens for the recreation of the residents.

1. T. Tang, *The Victorian Suburbanisation of Glasgow* (provisional title of forthcoming doctoral thesis), Department of Architecture and Building Science, University of Strathclyde.

Fig. 2 *Clarendon Place, from the feuing plan of the lands of South Park belonging to W. S. Nisbet Esq., 1839.*
courtesy of Glasgow City Archives

Figure 2 is a vignette taken from the plan for the South Park estate, located to the north-west of Garnet Hill and laid out for feuing in

1839 by the architect Alexander Taylor. The entrance from St. George's Cross was to be marked by twin porticoes in the manner of Edinburgh's Waterloo Place. Only one was built, and it has survived. Building progressed according to plan only as far as the great garden circus at the heart of the scheme. After some hiatus the area was redeveloped to meet the emerging demand for cheaper, rented, tenement accommodation.

It happened that, for various reasons, all of the neo-classical schemes failed or were abandoned before the attempt. To give but one further example for the moment: in 1834, the main landowner south of the river, Sir John Maxwell of Pollok, proposed for his lands of Kinninghouse (next to Tradeston) a scheme that incorporated crescents and a vast circus, over 1000 feet in diameter, arranged on a curving east-west axis. The scheme was worked up in precise architectural form, but it came to nothing as these parts were absorbed into the infrastructure of an increasingly busy dockland.

After Maxwell's development interests shifted further south to Pollokshields his architect, David Rhind, produced, in 1849, a curious hybrid layout in which neo-classical elements – axial arrangements of circus, crescent and square, defined by palace-form architecture – are juxtaposed with curvilinear ribbons of detached villas (Fig. 3). It was, significantly, the villas that were built, not the terraces, while the east side of the estate was given over to tenements, the first dating from 1855.

The alternative offered to the neo-classicist vision was that of the Picturesque – either in the form of the arcadian villa or of the terrace as a country house, set apart in palatial symmetry in a scene of meadows, woods and distant mountains – here depicted in a vignette from a feuing plan for Kelvinside (Fig. 4). For the landowner the selling points were then what they are today in any suburban venture. One advertisement[2] for an estate to the east of the city features the 'natural beauty' and command of a view of the site which, it says, offers the advantages of 'suburban quiet' and

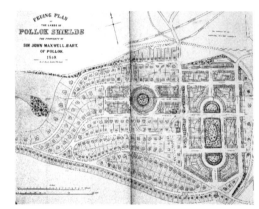

Fig. 3 *Feuing plan for Pollokshields, 1849.* courtesy of Glasgow City Archives.

Fig. 4 *Vignette from the Feuing Plan of Queenstown, Kelvinside, c. 1849.* courtesy of Glasgow City Archives.

2. The Glasgow Herald, 14 September 1857.

3. The Glasgow Herald, 31 January and 21 February 1870, quoted in M. A. Simpson and T. A. Lloyd (eds.), 1977, *Middle Class Housing in Britain*, Newton Abbot: David and Charles.

an 'open, healthful and retired residence' though still being within easy reach of the 'business ... of the town'. Another[3], for an estate to the west offers a 'mostly elevated' site, 'encouraging good air' and 'commanding fine views' over 'undulating and beautifully wooded [countryside] ... a landscape', it says, that is 'truly picturesque [and] seldom obtained in Suburban Dwellings'.

The drumlins rising gently from the Clydesdale plain, particularly those clustered north of the river and to the west of the city, were well suited for development according to this picturesque aesthetic. But to be successful the more outlying estates would first require improved access to the places of business, shopping and entertainment located in the city centre. New thoroughfares and improvements to existing country roads were promoted through Parliament by the landowners of the interested properties. A 'Skeleton Map of the West End' dated 1839 (Fig. 5) shows the new and improved routes emanating from St. George's Cross. 'New City Road' (now Maryhill Road) runs north-west to form a new route to Garscube, while Great Western Road takes its now undeviating path to the lands beyond the River Kelvin.

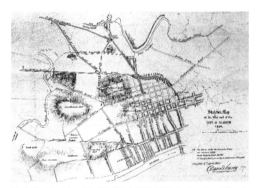

Fig. 5 *Skeleton Map of the West End, 1839*, Hill Collection, Royal Faculty of Procurators

There were over 20 estates competing in the development of what we now know as the West End of Glasgow, though at the time most were outwith the jurisdiction of the municipality. Looking in some detail at the three neighbouring estates of Hillhead, Kelvinside and Dowanhill, we find varying approaches in their initial plans and, consequently, quite different kinds of response to the developing economy of Victorian Glasgow.

The case of Hillhead illustrates the impact of road improvement on the fortunes of an estate. It had, optimistically, been prepared for feuing by the surveyor, David Smith, as early as the 1820s. Smith simply laid down an orthogonal grid of streets untrammelled over the contours of the hill. It would be a mistake, however, to read into the appearance of the grid here an intention to develop Hillhead on built-up Blythswood lines. Part of the estate was advertised in 1833, but it was not until after the opening of Great Western Road at the end of the decade that the business began to take off. The first new buildings to appear were villas. The development gained momentum with a change of owner who exploited the *laissez-faire* nature of the grid. By the time of the first Ordnance Survey (1860) (Fig. 6), as well as villas there were rows of two and three storeyed houses and tenements, all disposed without apparent order in the matrix of the grid.

Hillhead was exceptional among the suburban estates in that, as far as we know, the feuing plan and its architectural development were not conceived as one. That, and the openness of the grid, made it wholly flexible in response to the varied and changing demands of the increasingly populous city. In other cases, feuing plans and documents were quite specific about the type of development to be allowed, and frequently specified the architectural treatment to be observed. And in every such case the plans had to be modified to a greater or lesser extent. The initial proposals might be too ambitious, or too inflexible, or they might misjudge the demand for a particular kind of development.

The need for flexible planning is well illustrated by the history of the largest of these estates in the west, Kelvinside. Immediately after the estate changed hands in 1840, a feuing plan was commissioned from Decimus Burton who, after his early work on villas and terraces for Nash's Regent's Park, had gone on to provide designs for a number of estates in England.

The scheme that Burton produced for Kelvinside incorporated the Botanic Gardens and the Observatory, both recently relocated here from sites nearer the city centre. As to residences, almost the entire estate, both north and south of the Kelvin, is covered with an informal layout of commodious villas, over two hundred of them, each detached in its own landscaped garden. Arcadian settlements of this kind were, at this time, becoming familiar outgrowths of prosperous towns and cities in England but they had yet to establish

Fig. 6 *Hillhead in 1860*. Ordnance Survey

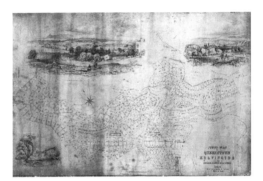

Fig. 7 *Feuing Plan of Queenstown, Kelvinside,* c. 1840. courtesy of Glasgow City Archives.

4. The Glasgow Herald, 14 September 1857.

5. The Glasgow Herald, 27 October 1858.

themselves north of the border. A few terraces of various forms appear in different parts of the plan. They include a number of straight terraces parallel to Great Western Road which fit ill with the generally curvilinear nature of the rest of the scheme. As it turned out, these terraces were the only part built according to the plan (Fig. 7).

Even in this part, the uptake was slow. In the 1850s there was a change of direction. Burton's villa-dominated layout was scrapped and new designs were proposed by Charles Wilson, James Rochead and James Salmon, senior. It was Salmon who received the commission. He had recently produced a scheme for the east-side suburb of Dennistoun. In the words of the advertisement, Dennistoun was to be 'planned on the best continental models'.[4] For 'continental' we can read Neo-Classical. It should be noted that almost nothing of this ambitious proposal, with its axes, terraces, crescents and serried rows of villas, was carried over into the later development of the estate.

The Kelvinside proprietors adopted a similar, and similarly unrealisable, grand plan from Salmon in their attempt to promote their fortunes. Burton's sparse distribution of villas with gardens was to be replaced by a supposedly more profitable layout of terraces with extensive communal pleasure-grounds. In Salmon's scheme Great Western Road is cut diametrically through two great circuses. The larger has concentric inner and outer terraces measuring 'over a quarter of a mile in circumference', according to a contemporary commentary.[5] Elsewhere, terraces are laid out on grids, barely inflected to the contours or the irregular boundary of the estate.

The final stage in the development of Kelvinside was marked by the abandonment of any kind of grand unifying plan, be it arcadian, picturesque, Neo-Classical or a combination from the three. Around 1870, a large part of the estate was feued or sold off in separate packages. Each parcel was developed to its own plan within certain

requirements as to size, height and quality laid down by the estate
superiors. One parcel, in which Alexander Thomson may have had
a commercial interest, was fronted by his two grandest terraces;
another, nearby, was given over mostly to large villas in their own
half-acre steadings; yet another revived the hierarchical formalisms
of neo-classicism.

This history demonstrates how, in pursuit of the elite housing
market, development strategies for Kelvinside underwent abrupt
conceptual changes. But, unlike many other landowners, the
Kelvinside Estate Company was able to maintain, for the most part,
its initial intention that the estate was 'to be occupied solely by
dwelling-houses of a superior description'[6], albeit at a cost of
decades of stagnation. Elsewhere, projects that aimed at the higher
end of the market were necessarily abbreviated, or were modified
to accommodate residents from lower social strata.

6. The Glasgow Herald, 2 October 1840, quoted in M. A. Simpson and
T. A. Lloyd (eds.), op. cit.

There was only one estate where the need for different *kinds* of
housing for a wide spectrum of society was recognised from the
outset. Dowanhill, contiguously south of Kelvinside and stretching
down to Partick, was acquired in separate lots by the entrepreneur
T. L. Paterson. Some authorities give the date as 1850, though the
estate papers show 1852. Incidentally, the same authorities,
including the authors of the Glasgow volume in *The Buildings of
Scotland* series, credit the feuing plan to the architect, James
Thomson, though in 1850 Thomson was only 15 years old.

The first feuing plan for Dowanhill that I know of is dated 1853 and
was by a land surveyor called James Smith (Fig. 8). The illustration
shows the central part of it. With one important exception, the main
features of the development as it was to be realised are all there.
Smith had an eye to the varying advantages of the site. Over the
undulating uplands around the observatory, he disposed villas and
terraces for the well-to-do. On the plain, towards Partick, he laid
down an orthogonal grid for tenements. Between these distinct
parts of the estate the plan provides the buffer of a small public

Fig. 8 *Feuing Plan for Dowanhill, 1853*, Hill Collection, Royal Faculty
of Procurators

Fig. 9 *Crown Circus, 1858*. Peter Reed

park and locates the church, and the communal meeting ground. All these features were carried into the construction of the estate, which proceeded slowly over the next 60 years or so. There was, as I have indicated, one significant change to the plan – and it is here that James Thomson more certainly enters the story. On the most elevated part of the estate – Dowanhill itself – the two rows of villas of Smith's plan were replaced by a circuit of outward-looking terraces. The reasons, no doubt, were economic; but the change also gave the developers the opportunity to construct a prominent advertisement for their new development. Accordingly, the convex summitry of Crown Circus, with one of the most refined elevations among Glasgow's classical terraces, was among the first of the buildings to be realised on site (Fig. 9).

Apart from this important revision, the Dowanhill development was realised more or less in the terms in which it had first been envisaged. Whereas other suburban estates were initiated with plans broadly conceived for a limited sector of society, on Dowanhill different forms of housing were deployed for a range of social groups. Hence, better than others, it could respond to changes in patterns of demand. Particularly, in providing for tenement development near to the developing manufacturing base of Partick, Smith foreshadowed the emerging relationship between the West End and the city as a whole.

By 1860 at the time of the first Ordnance Survey (Fig. 10), most of the estates to the west of the city had entered the competitive market. The overall picture was one of disconnected initiatives holding no promise of a coherent urban structure. What was to transform the situation in the second half of the 19th century and was to give Glasgow its definitive urban image, was widespread speculation in housing for the emerging artisan class. Invariably this housing was in the form of tenements.

In most of the suburban estates, schemes based upon the terrace and the villa were abbreviated, or modified, or rebuilt on tenement lines, or not progressed at all beyond some exploratory stage. The interstices between the existing scattering of enclaves were filled in, for the most part, with tenements, and tenements appeared along the thoroughfares that had opened up the countryside for colonisation. It was the tenement, therefore, that amalgamated and enveloped the disparate enterprises of the estates, bringing with it the density and variety of population necessary to sustain the amenities of urban, rather than suburban, living. For economic reasons, almost all of this tenement development was to some variation on the gridded theme – so this story, which began with reactions against the grid, ends with its prevalence throughout the expanding city.

Next page: Fig. 10 *The West End of Glasgow in 1860.* Ordnance Survey

The Neo-Classical Town in Late Victorian and Early 20th-Century Scotland
Gavin Stamp

'Mutules in the cornice,
Acanthus round the door,
Grilles across the windows
Three feet from the floor.
Georgian in the country,
Neo-Grec in town,
That's the stuff to give 'em
If you want renown.'

Such was English *avant-garde* architectural fashion in the early 20th century as entertainingly defined by the architect Stanley Ramsay – who knew what he was talking about. In London and in certain other cities in England in the years immediately before and after the Great War the vogue was certainly for what was (and is) imprecisely described as 'Neo-Grec', a revival of the urbane elegance of the Regency Greek Revival – what might be called neo-neo-classicism. It was a particular expression of a European-wide desire for simplicity and order after years of license which preceded the advent of the Modern Movement and which, in the German-speaking countries, resulted in a revival of the Biedermeier.

In England, this revival was actively promoted by two schools of architecture: the Architectural Association under Robert Atkinson and the Liverpool School under Charles Reilly, both of whom designed buildings themselves in a 'Neo-Grec' style and reformed their schools on Beaux-Arts principles as filtered through American publications. The landmarks in this revival are such things as the published volumes of *The Liverpool Architectural Sketch Book* (1910, 1911, 1913, 1920), in which measured drawings of precedents like St. George's Hall can be found next to designs for new public buildings in a 'Neo-Grec' style, as well as the realisation of such designs as Richardson & Gill's New Theatre in Manchester of 1912. Most important of all, perhaps, was the completion of a major portion of the Duchy of Cornwall Estate in Kennington in South London, designed by Stanley Adshead and his partner, the author of the verse quoted earlier, Stanley Ramsay.

Previous page: Fig. 1 *Duchy of Cornwall Estate, Kennington, London, by Adshead & Ramsay*

Courtenay Square and the adjacent buildings represented the completed revolution of a wheel turning full circle, for the buildings are revivals of the hitherto-despised humble stock-brick urban terraces of Regency London, but interpreted with subtlety and intelligence. They were completed in the fateful year 1914, a year which also saw the publication of Albert Richardson's great illustrated book on *Monumental Classic Architecture in Great Britain and Ireland during the Eighteenth and Nineteenth Centuries*. The significance of this is that, after the long interval created by the Gothic Revival, the 'Queen Anne' movement and the eclectic Renaissance revival of the Late Victorians, the work of such neo-classicists as Soane, Cockerell, Smirke, Elmes and, indeed, Thomas Hamilton, W. H. Playfair and 'Greek' Thomson was taken seriously again.

From an English perspective, what makes Scotland different is that such a revival, such a reaffirmation of the principles of the last phase of the continuous classical tradition, would seem to have been considerably less necessary. For in Scotland the classical tradition never died. The Gothic Revival, although evident, was never as powerful as it was in England owing to the lack of a theological connection between Presbyterianism and Pointed architecture, and while the anti-classical romanticism of neo-Medieval aspiration encouraged a national expression in Baronial, and the early Renaissance eclecticism of the 1890s closely parallels developments south of the Border, a serious grammatical classicism continued to flourish. Such buildings as, say, St. Andrew's Halls in Glasgow of 1873–7 (Fig. 2) and the Kelvinside Academy of 1877–9, both designed by James Sellars, could not possibly have been built in England at the same time (although there is the sublime aberration of James Hibbert's Harris Library and Museum of 1882–93 in Preston).

It might be expected, therefore, that the return to the austere monumentality and the urbanity of the early 19th-century Greek Revival would have been even more pronounced in Scotland in the

Fig. 2 *St. Andrew's Halls, Glasgow, by James Sellars, 1873-77.*
Photograph, Gavin Stamp

early 20th century. Yet, puzzlingly and paradoxically, this does not seem to be the case. Both Edinburgh and Glasgow could, surely, have witnessed a highly creative and appropriate revival of or continuation of their urban traditions. With its orderly terraced façades, in which orthogonal regularity was humanised by topography, Edinburgh New Town provided the finest model of coherent urban development in Britain, yet new expansions to the city were either random assemblies of villas or suburban plans inspired by English low-density garden-city ideals.

In Glasgow the urban style established by Alexander Thomson continued to be followed in the late 19th century, with his former partner Robert Turnbull, amongst others, recycling his stock of motifs. Nevertheless, the tradition seems to have begun to wither by the beginning of the new century and the Langside Hill Church, designed in 1894–6 by Thomson's old assistant, Alexander Skirving, was in fact the last neo-classical church to be built in the city. Even so, with the waning of the Mackintosh influence after 1900 and the growing praise of Thomson's work in the (English) architectural press – Reginald Blomfield in the *Architectural Review* in 1904, Lionel Budden (of Liverpool) in *The Builder* in 1910, Trystan Edwards in the *Architect's and Builder's Journal* as well as Albert Richardson in 1914 – a revival of interest in Thomson's expressive urban Neo-Classical formulae might have been expected in Glasgow as in England. When the late John Summerson first visited the city in 1926 all he looked at were Thomson's buildings[1], yet there is little evidence that Glasgow students and architects were making creative use of these local paradigms.

There are exceptions to this generalisation. One is as extraordinary as it is good, for in St. Andrews in 1923, Paul Waterhouse designed Younger Hall, the students' union in North Street, in a crisp and austere Neo-Classical manner which pays tribute to Playfair and Thomas Hamilton, even Greek Thomson, while the absence of crowning cornices on the wings flanking the raised portico together with the use of fenestration with narrow side-lights (albeit a feature

1. See John Summerson's introduction to G. Stamp & S. McKinstry, eds, *'Greek' Thomson*, 1994.

of the 1820s) gives this academic temple of flavour of Art Deco *moderne*. This building – supremely unresponsive as it is to the *genius loci* of the ancient Scottish university – along with that of 1914–16 in East Port, Dunfermline, also by Waterhouse, looks as if it had emerged from the pages of *The Liverpool Architectural Sketch Book*. And the architect of both, of course, was English: the son of the formidable Alfred.

No 20th-century Neo-Classical building in Edinburgh is this good, although William Kininmonth's defiance of the *zeitgeist* in his façade of Adam House of 1954-5 deserves honourable mention. But at least the classical language was used with dignity and restraint in the capital whenever a public building was required between the wars, as with the 'grim Neo-Georgian'[2] Sheriff Court of 1934–7 by the Office of Works and the flattened stripped classical monumentality of Reginald Fairlie's National Library of Scotland, designed in 1934 and completed in 1955.

Nevertheless, the great Scottish cities which produced Playfair and a wave of Hamiltons, Thomson and Stark – and, for that matter, Archibald Simpson and John Smith – signally failed in the early 20th century to respond to an international Neo-Classical revival by building on that legacy. This may, in part, reflect the economic difficulties, but it is more the consequence of contemporary Scottish aspirations. For while England was gradually discovering Georgian as the authentic national classical vernacular, Scotland was looking to the tower houses and castles of the 16th and 17th centuries as the basis of a national style. And those of a more rigorous classical bent who were not content to follow Lorimer and others in this direction looked not to Scottish Neo-Classicism, but to France – and across the Atlantic. This, I think, is the answer to the problem.

As I have already argued, the Neo-Classical revival in England had much to do with certain schools of architecture reorganising themselves on Beaux-Arts lines – but at one remove and against a background of ignorance and amateurism. Scotland, in contrast,

2. *Buildings of Scotland* volume on *Edinburgh*: I would not call this building 'Neo-Georgian'.

had direct experience of Beaux-Arts methods of teaching and design through the architects who trained in Paris in the 1870s and 1880s and whose careers David Walker has exhaustively charted.[3]

This phase begins with J. J. Burnet, who studied at the atelier Pascal in 1875-7 and it was Burnet who became the most intelligent and sophisticated interpreter of the classical tradition in Scotland in the late Victorian and Edwardian decades.

Burnet created two of the most distinguished classical façades to be found in the grid-iron street-scape of Glasgow: the now lost Sauchiehall Street front of the Institute of Fine Arts of 1878 and that of the Athenaeum in St. George's Place, of 1886 (Fig 3). These were more accomplished, more grammatical and more inventive than any equivalent work in England even of a decade later, and Burnet's grasp of essentials makes the Edwardian Baroque of the south seem as vulgar as it is amateurish. Yet Burnet had a taste for sculptural effects which can be called baroque (or mannerist) and he seems to have learned little from the rectilinear austerity of Thomson's Glasgow. Curiously, his most accomplished essay in Neo-Classicism is not in Scotland at all but in London, where – having, alas, been tempted south in 1904 – he added to Smirke's Greek Revival British Museum with rare brilliance and sympathy. Nevertheless, his McGeoch's warehouse in Glasgow 1905-10 (Fig. 4) – whose disappearance is one of the city's worst architectural losses – showed a neo-classical delight in monumental trabeation as an expression of the steel frame, but given individuality by a mannerist-cum-art nouveau flavour.

Burnet did, however, have an indirect influence on the eventual, and short-lived, adoption of a monumental neo-classicism in the streets of Glasgow, for he was instrumental in the appointment of Eugène Bourdon in 1904 as the first Professor of Architecture. This was a significant *coup*, for while Reilly, Atkinson and others affected familiarity with Parisian methods, Bourdon was the real thing: a real live Beaux-Arts-trained Frenchman. Furthermore, he had –

3. David Walker, *Scotland and Paris: 1874–1887* in John Frew & David Jones (eds.), *Scotland and Europe: Architecture & Design 1850–1940*, St Andrews Studies in the History of Scottish Architecture & Design, 1991.

Fig. 3 *Athenaeum, St. George's Place, Glasgow, by J. J. Burnet, 1886*

Fig. 4 *McGeoch's Warehouse, Glasgow, by J. J. Burnet, 1905-10 (demolished).* RCAHMS

4. For Bourdon, see Gavin Stamp, 'Mackintosh, Burnet and Modernity' in The Age of Mackintosh: Architectural Heritage III, the Journal of the Architectural Heritage Society of Scotland, 1992.

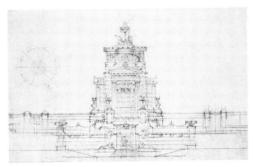

Fig. 5 'A Mausoleum in a Nobleman's Park', student design by J. M. Whitlaw, 1909. In: Designs in Architecture by James Mitchell Whitelaw

5. Alan Powers, 'Edwardian Architectural Education: A Study of three Schools of Architecture' in AA Files no.5, January 1984, pp. 56–9.

6. Designs in Architecture by James Mitchell Whitelaw (1886–1913), 1916, in which the 'Memoir' by 'A.G.S.' (presumably A . G. Shoosmith) notes that this tragic victim of drowning at Bournemouth had been a pupil of Thomson's assistant, Alexander Skirving, 'who inspired him with a love of Greek art and brought him under the influence of the work of Alexander Thomson, an influence which he always felt strongly, and which is evident in many of his designs'. Whitelaw then worked for Honeyman while studying at the Glasgow School of Art before, in 1907, joining Burnet in London to work on the King Edward VII Galleries.

Fig. 6 Elevation of former Union Bank of Scotland, St. Vincent Street, Glasgow, by Richard Gunn for James Miller, 1924. RIAS

7. For Miller, see Audrey Sloan with Gordon Murray, James Miller 1860–1947, RIAS, 1993.

apparently – spent time in New York detailing a classical steel-framed skyscraper. And that, in Edwardian Glasgow, was the acme of modernity and suggested the future direction of architecture. The tangible results of this American connection were to be seen in the streets of Glasgow in the decade after the Great War, and it is here, perhaps, that a modern Neo-Classical aesthetic can be identified.[4]

The pre-war projects of Bourdon's students are often French and frothy in character, although the best sometimes demonstrated an American monumentality. This is evident in the colonial Parliament House design of 1909–10 by Richard Gunn which, if built in Washington D.C. would look quite at home. Reilly's students in Liverpool were looking in the same direction but as Alan Powers, the historian of these schools, has written, 'Gunn's drawing, in particular, is superior in design and execution to any Liverpool work' and Powers notes that this student 'expressed a preference, unique at this date, for Louis Sullivan rather than for his over-trained Beaux-Arts contemporaries in America'.[5] Another Glaswegian student, J. M. Whitelaw (Fig. 5), whose terminal railway station design of 1913 won him the Soane Medallion, was a convinced Neo-Classicist who, apparently, was influenced by 'Greek' Thomson but his promising career was curtailed while bathing at Bournemouth in 1913.[6]

Like Reilly in Liverpool, Bourdon sent his best students to the U.S.A. and when Gunn returned to Glasgow he had learned much from those over-trained Beaux-Arts Americans. In 1918 he went to work for James Miller as chief assistant and must have had a considerable influence on the design of the magnificent head office of the Union Bank of Scotland (now the Bank of Scotland) in St. Vincent Street (Fig. 6). This building, won in competition in 1924, shows deep familiarity with the impressive commercial buildings of a decade earlier by firms like McKim, Mead & White and Holabird & Roche. The lack of concordance between the lower giant Ionic order and the height of the noble banking hall inside is distressing once noticed, but the building is magnificently executed and superbly detailed. It would look unexceptional in Detroit or Montreal.[7]

This bank was the grandest of a series of stone-clad steel-framed commercial structures of American character which rose in Glasgow over the next decade. All adopt a monumental, stripped classical trabeated treatment and use the American trick (taken up by Burnet in his influential Kodak House in London of 1910–11) of facing intervening floors in metal so the stone-faced stanchions between vertical strips of glazing read as a giant order. Greek Revival as well as Renaissance models inspired the American prototypes, so the use of an austere trabeated language to conceal and yet express the steel frame might be characterised as 'Neo-Classical'.

Several of these buildings were by Miller (or Gunn): the earlier and incomplete McLaren Warehouse of 1922–4 in George Square and the much more refined and abstracted Commercial Bank of Scotland on the corner of West Nile Street and West George Street of 1931 (Fig. 7). But the biggest chunk of America in Glasgow was raised in Bothwell Street, where the Scottish Legal Assurance Society building occupies a complete block. It was designed by E. G. Wylie of Wright & Wylie – who had been both a student and a lecturer at the Glasgow School of Architecture and was strongly influenced by Bourdon.[8] Built in 1927–31, its remorseless monumental double-pilastrade frame on each façade owes something to Burnet's Wallace Scott Factory of 1913 but, with its crowning cornice and refined classical detailing, the general effect is of Selfridge's brought north (although the authors of the *Buildings of Scotland* volume note a more recondite debt to Maurice Beresford's Cairo Telephone Exchange).

Close by is the finest of these American buildings: the Commercial Bank of Scotland (now Royal Bank of Scotland) on the corner of Bothwell Street and Wellington Street, built in 1934–5 (Fig. 8). It is again from the office of James Miller, who managed to produce a convincing design despite the early death of Richard Gunn in 1933. A three-storey abstracted and fluted pilastrade on the side elevation turns into an exotic Corinthian order with shaved bases on the narrow front. Most remarkable is the absence of a crowning

Fig. 7 *Former Commercial Bank of Scotland, West George and West Nile Streets, Glasgow, by James Miller, 1931.* Photograph Gavin Stamp

8. Biographical note in Andor Gomme and David Walker, *Architecture of Glasgow*, 1968, 1987.

cornice; instead there is a tall blank attic with set-backs, giving the whole building that abstracted exotic monumentalism typical of the 1930s. It is a building worthy of comparison with the work of that Franco-American Beaux-Arts modern classicist, Paul Cret.

No other city in Britain can boast a series of inter-war buildings as monumental, as classical and as American as those raised in Glasgow. Reilly's pupil Herbert Rowse brought his own experience of the Unites States to the streets of Liverpool in a series of magnificent commercial piles, but these do not really compare. Glasgow's American classical buildings work because they fit so well into the city's grid-iron plan, emphasising the transatlantic character of the city to which some pre-1914 buildings also contribute. The image, therefore – on this side of the Atlantic – of giant walls of stone and towering orders of pilasters defining rectilinear street lines is peculiarly Glaswegian. But it was a short-lived phase and was largely confined to the commercial heart of the city.

Fig. 8 *Elevation of former Commercial Bank of Scotland, Bothwell Street, 1934.* RCAHMS

9. Minutes and report on the Tolbooth Steeple etc. published by the Corporation of Glasgow, 1915, illustrating the Honeyman & Keppie proposals.

The only attempt to go beyond the grid and to achieve monumental Beaux-Arts, or 'City Beautiful' town planning in Glasgow at this time was a misguided proposal to improve the historic core of the medieval city at Glasgow Cross. Following a fire in the Tontine Hotel in 1911, a competition to replan this strategic junction was won in 1914 by Honeyman & Keppie who proposed to continue the Haussmanising of this decayed part of the city by rounding off the streetline at the bottom of the High Street and rebuilding the Tron Steeple as an isolated landmark to close the vista down Trongate (Fig.9).[9] In the event the city decided against moving this tower while weightier matters postponed realisation of the scheme until 1922, by which date Mackintosh's colourless supplanter, Graeme Henderson, had changed it into something much more ambitious.

Fig. 9 *'Glasgow Cross Alterations'*. Perspective looking north of competition winning scheme by Graeme Henderson of Honeyman & Keppie, 1914. RCAHMS

The buildings at the bottom of the High Street were now to be replaced by two concave blocks to leave the Tolbooth Steeple as a free-standing monument in the centre of a new classical crescent, formed by flaccid new blocks with an elevated and continuous Ionic order. In the event, only the north-western quadrant block was built, together with the Mercat building to the east which sports a grand exhedra inspired by that of the American-designed Bush House at the bottom of Kingsway in London. No more was done; the steeple was left forlorn and meaninglessly detached while the area was further impoverished by removing the equestrian statue of King Billy from Trongate. This is the sort of development which rightly gives the Beaux-Arts a bad name – although compared with what Mr. Bruce, the city engineer, and subsequent planners achieved in Glasgow after the Second World War – when delight of vistas and axes had been transmuted into worship of wide roads and roundabouts – it may well seem urbane and tactful (Fig.10).

Fig. 10 *View of Glasgow Cross in 1994 looking east towards Mercat Building.* Photograph Gavin Stamp

This essay is largely concerned with Glasgow which I know best, but I am aware that similar tendencies can be detected in other Scottish cities. In Dundee a new civic centre was commenced with the erection of the Roman Doric colonnade of the Caird Hall by James Thomson, planned in 1914, completed in 1922 and soon flanked by Burnet's City Chambers and a balancing range opposite, but, unfortunately, the creation of this axial forum required the removal of William Adam's Town House. In Perth an ambitious if mediocre new city hall was begun while here in Aberdeen the additions to the Art Gallery followed by the erection of the War Memorial Cowdray Hall in 1923–5 by Marshall Mackenzie resulted in a monumental and grand complex of classical civic buildings.

Even so, these gestures seem of little consequence compared with the grand civic buildings and planning achieved in England in the years after the Great War – Bradshaw Gas & Hope's Le Mans Crescent in Bolton, for instance – while in Glasgow the American-inspired Neo-Classicism of the 1920s made no real contribution to urban planning and none at all to domestic design. The possibilities for coherent and civilised urban development offered by Alexander Thomson and other 19th-century Neo-Classicists were not developed in these monuments of commerce. But then the civilised lessons

Fig. 11 *Edinburgh Police telephone kiosk.* Photograph Gavin Stamp

provided by Adshead & Ramsay's work in Kennington were largely ignored by the English, so Scotland was not especially blinkered.

The irony is that the design in Scotland which most closely corresponds to the neo-Regency ideal defined in Stanley Ramsay's verse is to be found not in Glasgow but in Edinburgh, although it could equally well have graced the Duchy of Cornwall Estate in London. I refer, of course, to that model of sensitive urbanity and elegant detailing, the Edinburgh police telephone kiosk designed by the city architect, Ebenezer MacRae, and his assistants, A. Rollow and J. A. Tweedie, in 1931–33. This exquisite piece of modern street furniture cunningly disguised as a Regency sentry box really can be described as neo-Neo-Classical (Fig. 11).

**Modernity, Urbanity and Rationalism:
New Towns of the 20th Century**
Miles Glendinning

The previous papers in this book are mostly concerned with concepts of urban development of a dense, even monumental character; they trace a national and international tradition which stretched from the classicism of the 18th century and earlier, through the massed tenement building of the late 19th, and on into the early 20th century. And more recently, in the 1980s, the theme has once again been taken up, now by post-Modern advocates of classical urban 'interventions'.

The focus of this paper is rather different: it is concerned with the five government-planned new towns built in Scotland following the passing of the 1946 New Towns Act: East Kilbride (designated 1947), Glenrothes (1948), Cumbernauld (1955), Livingston (1962) and Irvine (1966). These projects developed out of a concept which, at first glance, diverged sharply from the traditions discussed in the previous chapters of this book: a concept, invented in the late 1880s by Theodor Fritsch and Ebenezer Howard and greatly expanded after 1945, which envisaged new, *low*-density settlements intended to siphon off population from the dense cities. Today, even the name 'new town' seems to us anomalous, emphasising the disparity with its late 18th-century Edinburgh predecessor. Even if we do not subscribe to the fierce post-Modern polarisation between the good traditional city and the bad new city, most of us today would certainly not regard the post-war new towns as examples of 'classicism' or 'neo-classicism'.

In this short paper, I cannot systematically describe the development and physical patterns of the five new towns. For basic facts and figures, readers should consult F. J. Osborn and A. Whittick's *New Towns: Their Origins, Achievements and Progress* (1977) – a book which presents a valuable compendium of statistical information (albeit interwoven with triumphalistic New Town propaganda). Here, I am concerned to discuss the values and the ideology of the new towns, and in particular to examine the specific issue of whether the values of the mid-20th-century new towns conflict with those of the Scottish 'urban tradition' examined in previous papers.

Previous page: Fig. 1 *The 'Replanning of Britain': Town and Country Planning Association meeting in London, 1944.* Frederic Osborn is seated at front left.

First, the 'case against', which can be summarised as follows. The
new towns are neither 'urban' nor 'Scottish'. They are not 'urban'
for a very obvious reason, namely that they are a Modernist
conception, which we in the post-Modern era categorise as 'anti-
urban'. The new towns programme coincided with the ascendancy
of the Modern Movement, and in some ways took to an extreme the
Modernist passion for vast, rationalistic re-ordering of human
activities in a spatially segregated manner, based on the assumption
that designers could exactly measure, and cater for, the needs of
human habitation, whether on the scale of a 'minimum kitchen' or
that of an entire 'regional plan'. These were entirely new
settlements designed not on the monumental, classical principles
of 19th-century planned towns but according to the open, abstract
spatial play of Modernism, and thus their conception is antagonistic
both to Neo-Classical urbanism, and to today's heterogeneous post-
Modern vision of myriad individual 'interventions', aimed at the
'reintegration' of 'the city in all its contradictory and even chaotic
essence' (Portoghesi).

Nor, our initial accusation continues, are the new towns 'Scottish'
– at any rate, from the viewpoint of today's ever-increasing stress
on national cultural sovereignty. Instead, they were part of a
homogenising 'British' movement to abolish dense Scottish housing
patterns and replace them with low-density English patterns. This
had begun before 1914 with the advocacy of leafy cottage garden
suburbs, and the labelling of Scottish housing, especially the
tenement, as 'inferior': the 'myth of bad Scottish housing'. After
1939 all that happened was that the British town and country
planning profession stepped up the assault to a large scale – leafy
overspill new towns versus dense outmoded Glasgow. The planners'
wartime-inspired, somewhat authoritarian philosophy envisaged
'strategic dispersal' to Garden City settlements across Britain.
Frederic Osborn, head of the Town and Country Planning
Association (Fig. 1) and arch-apostle of the new towns, reminded
Scots in 1938 that 'all British towns throughout history, whether
planned or unplanned, have begun by endeavouring to provide for

everybody a separate house and garden'; the tenement, 'always the last desperate resource', would finally be made obsolete by 'overspill' of population from Glasgow. And Osborn's chief Glasgow ally, Mrs Jean Mann, asked in 1949: 'The population of Scotland is over five million and one half are in the Clyde Valley. Why keep them there?'

However, as so often, historical fact is more complicated than this kind of crude hindsight-perspective. The building of Scottish new towns, rather than some alien Modernist imposition, was closely interrelated to what was going on in the 'old towns', and was tied in to a complex equation of concepts of the city, which in fact perpetuated and enriched the ideas discussed earlier. Just as John Lowrey argued in the case of Edinburgh's New Town, Scotland's 20th-century 'low-density' settlements, including both inter-war housing schemes and post-1945 new towns, likewise set out to complement rather than ignore or slight existing urban traditions.

In the remainder of this paper, I am going to trace some of the complications of this relationship, firstly by discussing the pre-history of the new towns' ideology at the turn of the century, and then by tracing the planned housing and urbanist projects which were actually implemented during the mid-20th century, including both the new towns themselves and other 'rival' building programmes of the same years.

Let us glance back at the turn of the century, when the ideals of establishing new Garden-City settlements separate from existing cities were first adumbrated in England and Germany. Two vital points about pre-1914 Scottish housing have been obscured by the 20th-century tradition of exclusive comparisons with English patterns, and the resulting rhetoric of Scottish 'inferior housing'. First, that a trend *away* from promiscuous urban denseness was a central element in the pre-war mainstream of Scottish urban reformism (as it had been in the late 18th century, in the Edinburgh New Town). Second, that this Scottish anti-denseness movement,

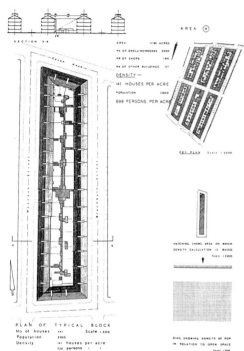

Fig. 2 *The 'problem'*: Diagram prepared in 1945 for the Clyde Valley Plan, showing the densest type of 19th-century Glasgow tenemental layout. The 'perimeter' disposition of the blocks contrasts with the far more intense exploitation of sites common on the Continent. Scottish Development Department

in turn, formed a part – a highly progressive part – of a wide international movement of housing and urban innovation among 'tenemental' European countries. If we, for instance, compare Scottish late 19th-century tenement with the colossally overcrowded, deep-plan *Mietskaserne* of Germany, the perimeter layouts and segregated internal house plans of Scottish tenements seem, in sanitary-reform terms, highly 'progressive' (Fig.2). And the housing reformist debates of Glasgow, or Geddes' efforts in Edinburgh, closely parallel the balanced policies of tenement reform, 'artistic' slum-clearance and garden cities of cottages attempted in pre-1914 Rome or many German cities. Thus we should not be distracted by the anglocentric rhetoric of some early 20th-century Scottish Garden-City propagandists, into overlooking the wider national and European precedents of their anti-tenement, pro-cottage ideology.

But what happened once the concept, or myth, of Scottish 'inferior housing' took hold, in the wake of the first and second World Wars? Did this lead to a more radical schism from older urban patterns? The answer seems to have been only a partial affirmative; for elements of 'tenemental' denseness continued to thrive – even in the new towns themselves. Inter-war municipal housing had certainly begun with a determined attempt to break from the tenement. But the rhetoric of 'inferior Scottish housing' soon rebounded against the cottage protagonists by fanning a popular demand for higher and higher output, which could not be met at low density. Largely to boost output, there was a gradual reversion to flatted patterns, with three-storey tenements of basically neo-classical character built on urban sites and two-storey flats in peripheral locations. This counter-trend was bolstered by a new, sharper patriotic rhetoric of 'Scottish tradition' in housing, unleashed by Lorimer in a 1928 address as RIAS President (in which he demanded the massed building of 'large blocks of flats' in the suburbs), and by increasing admiration among architects for the new and visually varied patterns of flatted mass housing being built in some continental countries.

And the same tendency – the gradual reassertion of elements of dense Scottish urbanism – emerged even after 1945, when the new town movement got underway. At first, the planning faction, the faction of low-density overspill, seemed ascendant, and set to curb the big municipalities' revived flat-building. Their first big victory was the government's endorsement, in 1946, of Abercrombie and Matthew's *Clyde Valley Regional Plan*, which called for Glasgow Corporation to be hemmed in by a green belt and for new towns to be built (Fig. 3); the first new town, East Kilbride, was designated the following year. From then on, the new town and overspill programme prospered, with the aid of special government subsidies, able to pick and choose skilled workers and tenants, and to exclude the unskilled and the poor. In this circular way, East Kilbride proved, economically and socially, a great 'success'. The other of the first two new towns, Glenrothes, had nothing to do with overspill utopianism, but set out to knit together a semi-rural mining area of Fife. It was inspired by another key post-war plan, very different in philosophy from the confrontational Clyde Valley blueprint: Frank Mears's Central and South-East Plan, which set out a Geddes-like vision of regional nucleations of existing settlements.

But even on Clydeside, things soon began to diverge from the planners' prescription. In East Kilbride (Fig. 4), 36% of the new dwellings were flats. Osborn exasperatedly scolded: 'It may be that in Scotland it is just a little difficult to shake off the tradition of flat building'. Even in this anti-municipal stronghold, municipal-style pressures for housing output were emerging. In the 1960s and '70s the original population target (45,000) was progressively stepped up to 70,000, then 100,000. In 1963, East Kilbride was elevated to burgh status: a range of large municipal projects was commenced, notably a civic centre and Alec Buchanan Campbell's huge Dollan Baths (1965–8, Fig.5). And it is also important to note that the regional planning movement in Scotland after 1945 took on marked overtones of administrative devolution – a strategy chartered by the same wartime Secretary of State, Tom Johnston, who had set the Clyde Valley Plan study in motion.

Fig. 3 *The 'cure'.* Perspective prepared by Alan Reiach for the Clyde Valley Plan, showing proposed low-density modern housing pattern for future Clydeside satellite towns. Note the combination of openness and greenery with elements of modern 'urbanity', especially the use of blocks of flats as vertical punctuations. Scottish Development Department

Fig. 4 *East Kilbride New Town (designated 1947).* Aerial view of town centre (at left centre) and nearby areas. The highly segregated plan, with 'neighbourhood units' separated from each other and the centre by roads or greenery, is clearly visible; the Clyde Valley Plan concept of low-density housing punctuated by medium-height flats was upheld here, with the addition of several high 'point blocks' for higher income residents. RCAHMS

Fig. 5 *East Kilbride: the daring 324 ft. concrete parabolic arch roof of the Dollan Baths (architect: A. Buchanan Campbell),* seen when new, in 1968

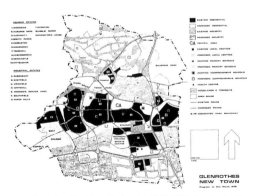

Fig. 6 *Glenrothes New Town (designated 1948).* 1976 plan showing the dispersed neighbourhood unit layout. Glenrothes Development Corporation

Away from the new towns, in the old municipal centres, above all in Glasgow, there was an even more emphatic move back to flat-building. But this was an ideologically ambiguous matter, as the new developments took a novel form – Modern architecture – which in some ways did seem to resemble the new town formula, and to diverge from older patterns of the city; for they, too, insisted on open, airy planning on a large utopian scale. But this was combined with a taste for large monumental, rectilinear groups of buildings in urban contexts, which in some ways chimed in with the neo-classical urbanism of the previous century. Modernist architects would have heartily agreed with Osborn on the undesirability of the old tenement, but their replacement for it was even larger in scale! Even in the 1930s, one of the key elements in that decade's 'renewal' of tenement building had already been an admiration for Continental Modernism, including tall blocks – a concept promoted vigorously by the young Robert Matthew, who, in the late 1930s and early 1940s, had helped create a new, government-based establishment of social building and planning in Scotland.

By the 1950s, Modernism was accepted in principle by everyone involved in the Scottish housing-planning 'nexus', and the result was great complexity in conceptions of the 'urban'. This architectural complexity paralleled and interacted with a complexity in patronage and policy, which stemmed from a sharpening rivalry in housing production between the established municipalities and the 'overspill' or 'anti-municipal' grouping (the latter including the new towns and the government-controlled Scottish Special Housing Association). Within Glasgow itself, high blocks on Modernist, open-planned lines were built by three rival factions within the Corporation. The first of these was a technocratic group led by chief Glasgow Corporation planner Ron Nicoll, who tried to help the overspill programme by starting a programme of designer-controlled multi-storey 'comprehensive development areas' within the city, beginning with Hutchesontown/Gorbals (from 1956); these were of strictly limited density and designed to precipitate mass overspill. The second was a somewhat populist group of opponents of overspill, led by the corporation's firebrand housing convener, Bailie David Gibson, who tried to block overspill by building 'package-deal' tower blocks supplied by contractors on any available gap site. And the third was a job-protection initiative by the corporation's own direct labour force, who engaged the architect Sam Bunton to design daring, steel-framed 31-storey tower blocks that their workforce could build in rivalry with Gibson's package-deal-contractors.

All these programmes, although mutually hostile in policy terms, in fact had a lot in common in their physical and social aspects. They represented a big cut in density compared with the 19th-century tenements, but achieved a sense of place through monumental big blocks. Socially, they continued the older pattern of retention of poorer people in 'inner' areas (which was now defined as the city as a whole) and out-migration of the better off (now defined as the overspill of skilled workers). But whereas the 19th-century poor had been housed in tumbledown, subdivided old houses, the giant modern blocks made new dwellings, mod. cons. and 'private' dwelling space available to even the poorest citizens.

And in the new towns, too, the Modernism of the 1960s stimulated an equally complex and, on the whole, 'urban' orientation in planning. A fresh generation of modern new town designers was now beginning to reject the entire early Modernist emphasis on open space and segregated uses, whether in the Garden-City form of dispersed 'neighbourhood units' or in the form of the tower blocks of the two rival groups in Glasgow. Instead, they sought what they called 'urbanity'. At Cumbernauld, the model was 'The Italian Hill Town' (Figs. 7 and 8). Here, there was a much closer clustering of low dwellings integrated with clumps of point blocks and focused on Geoffrey Copcutt's hyper-urbanist tour-de-force of the town centre (from 1963, Fig. 10): a pioneer of the fantastic megastructure ideal, with multiple layers and uses juxtaposed in a single envelope – and a late Modernist equivalent of the multi-use 'bridge/street' concept outlined by Bill Brogden's earlier paper.

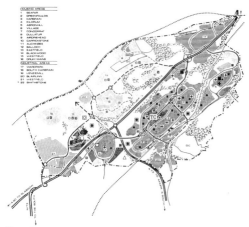

Fig. 7 *Cumbernauld New Town (designated 1955)*. 1975 outline plan, showing the original housing areas, closely encircling the hilltop town centre, and subsequent satellite areas. Cumbernauld Development Corporation

Fig. 8 *Cumbernauld New Town*. 1989 aerial photograph taken from north-west. In the foreground is the dramatically contoured Seafar housing area (built from 1961), with dense two-storey rows of split-level dwellings punctuated by 12-storey *Bison* blocks. In the middle is the original town centre, its strong alignment reflecting the roads that run through it. In the background is the Carbrain area, whose flatter site allowed a more regular layout of two-storey blocks. RCAHMS

Fig. 9 *Cumbernauld New Town, Town Centre Phase 1.* 1964 drawings by M. Evans. The complexity and juxtaposition of functions in this 'canonical megastructure' (Banham) created, on a previously empty site, a set-piece of the most intense late-Modernist urbanism. Cumbernauld Development Corporation

Thus, at the height of1960s Modernism, the new towns, far from being 'anti-urban' interlopers, were hotbeds of multi-faceted urbanism, evolving in a creative tension with other Modernist urban ideals in Glasgow and the big municipalities. The final two new towns, Livingston and Irvine, did revert, to some extent, to a less dense pattern: at Livingston, this was offset by rationalist elements such as a street-grid layout and an extensive use of precast concrete 'systems' (Fig. 10, next page). Conversely, recent overseas versions of the new town ideal have often taken a far higher-density form: for instance, in Hong Kong or Singapore.

Let us, finally, return briefly to the position today. These international Modernist trends and debates, in which Scotland played her distinctive part, seemed to become obsolete in the 1970s and 1980s, and were displaced by an equally international post-Modernist stress on 'regeneration' of existing cities and 'traditional' patterns. In this country, the change was symbolised in the reversal of the connotations of the word 'tenement' – from absolute dystopia to absolute Utopia. The aspiration of the town and country planners to reshape entire regions was abandoned in favour of a narrower focus on 'The City', an arena where all Modernist visions – Gibson's towers as much as the planners' new towns – were now labelled 'anti-urban'. This shift in priorities was dramatically heralded in 1975–6, within the new towns programme itself, following the achievement of one of the Clyde Valley planners' long-term aims: the setting up of an overarching regional authority. For one of the first acts of Strathclyde Regional Council was to abandon a planned sixth new town, at Stonehouse and redirect the resources allocated for it into 'GEAR', a huge Glasgow urban regeneration scheme.

So is there any possibility that we, burdened with all these preconceptions of our own, can reach an historical accommodation with the very different urbanist values of the Modernist post-war reconstruction efforts, including the new towns programme? Even if we do not subscribe to polemical anti-Modernist formulations which caricature an entire generation as corrupt or deluded, clearly we no longer accept unproblematically the claims of Modernism to 'rational' design in accordance with faith in material progress. And on the social front, although community remains as much an aim as ever in urbanist debates, we no longer accept the belief of that early post-war generation, which included both the Garden-City planners and the dense Modernists, that you *create* community by planning and providing new dwellings and settlements. Post-1968, post-Jane Jacobs, it is a basic tenet that community stems not from the providers but from the users, and from the preservation of supposedly 'traditional' patterns *against* change. But at the same time we do still have a surprising amount in common with Modernism. For instance, the very concept of the 'user' was invented by the Modernists, as part of their drive for exact measuring of 'needs' and 'standards' – and nobody today would actually give up the internal mod. cons. – bathroom, etc. – which were the focus of those 'standards' and which formed a central concern of the drive to build tower blocks. Has the rationalist urge disappeared altogether, or merely entered a new phase?

Fig. 10 *Livingston New Town (designated 1962)*. View from the Craigshill housing area under construction in 1965. Laing

These are all very complicated matters. All I can do now, in conclusion, is to return briefly to our theme today – the Neo-Classical town and its contemporary relevance. If the Neo-Classical town was characterised by rationalism as much as by romanticism, and if many people today are reacting against post-Modern urbanist ideology as anarchic and unprincipled, then the Modernist period of Scottish urban history, with its kaleidoscopic variety of rationalistic interpretations of the city, must surely be of some interest. But, of course, we must not stampede into another 180-degree turn and revive Modernism as a new golden age. The tradition of beginning each new phase of architectural or urbanist ideology by totally rubbishing your predecessor – a tradition invented in the 1830s by A. W. N. Pugin in England – has never completely caught on in this country. We tend to stress continuity more than confrontation, and so I suggest that the best way to look on Scotland's Modernist legacy, including new towns and tower blocks, is alongside, rather than in opposition to, the older patterns

BIBLIOGRAPHY

PRE-1945 HOUSING AND PLANNING:
I. H. Adams, *The Making of Urban Scotland*, 1978
W. H. Ballantine, *Rebuilding a Nation*, 1944
J. A. Bowie, *The Future of Scotland*, 1939
G. Cherry, *Pioneers in British Planning*, 1981 (Osborn, Geddes chapters)
S. Damer, *A Social History of Glasgow Council Housing*, 1991 (Mitchell Library)
T. Fritsch, *Die Stadt der Zukunft*, 1896
J. S. Gibson, *The Thistle and the Crown*, 1985
M. Horsey, *Tenements and Towers*, 1990
E. Howard, *Tomorrow: A Peaceful Path to Real Reform*, 1898
L. Paterson, *The Autonomy of Modern Scotland*, 1994
P. Reed (ed.), *Glasgow, the Forming of the City*, 1993
Royal Commission on the Housing of the Industrial Population of Scotland, Report, 1917 (Cd. 8731: the *Ballantyne Report*)
R. Roder (ed.), *Scottish Housing in the 20th Century*, 1989

POST-1945 PLANNING (GENERAL):
P. Abercrombie and R. H. Matthew, *The Clyde Valley Plan 1946*, 1949
J. S. Gibson, *The Thistle and the Crown*, 1985
R. Grieve, *Grieve on Geddes*, 1990
F. Mears, *Regional Survey and Plan for Central ... Scotland*, 1949
F. J. Osborn and A. Whittick, *New Towns*, 1977
Royal Commission on the Distribution of the Industrial Population, Report, 1940 (Cd. 6153: the *Barlow Report*)
Royal Town Planning Institute, *A Celebration of Planning in Scotland*, 1989
R. Saville (ed.), *Economic Development of Modern Scotland*, 1985
Scottish Council (Development and Industry), *Inquiry into the Scottish Economy*, 1961 (Toothill Report)
Scottish Development Department, *Central Scotland – a Programme for Development and Growth*, 1963
R. Smith and U. Wannop (eds.), *Strategic Planning in Action*, 1985

POST-1945 HOUSING (GENERAL):
T. Begg, *Fifty Special Years*, 1987
M. Glendinning and S.Muthesius, *Tower Block*, 1994 (chapters 20, 25)
R. Rodger (ed.), *Scottish Housing in the 20th Century*, 1989
Scottish Housing Advisory Committee, *Planning our New Homes*, 1944
R.Smith, *Multi-Dwelling Building in Scotland*, in A. Sutcliffe (ed.), Multi-storey Living, 1974

CUMBERNAULD NEW TOWN:
Architectural Design, May 1963 (Town Centre)
C. Carter and M. Keating, *The Designation of Cumbernauld New Town*, 1986

EAST KILBRIDE NEW TOWN:
R. Smith, *East Kilbride*, 1979

POSTWAR-GLASGOW:
R. Bruce, *First Planning Report to the Highways and Planning Committee of the Corporation of Glasgow*, 1945 (2 vols.)
Glasgow Corporation, *Report of Visit ... to the Marseilles Block*, 1954
Glasgow Corporation, *Report on ... Birmingham, Coventry, London*, 1955
A. G. Jury, *Glasgow's Housing Centenary*, 1966
M. Keating, *The City that Refused to Die*, 1988
P. Reed (ed), *Glasgow, the Forming of the City*, 1993

of tenements and villa suburbs: not as a pathological aberration, but as one dramatic phase in a richly variegated pattern of urban history.

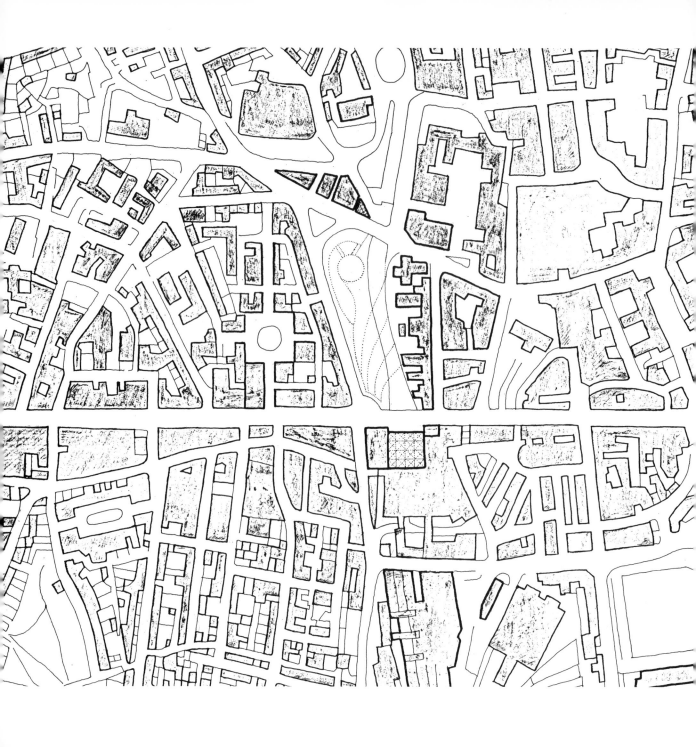

The Denburn: Aberdeen's Past and Aberdeen's Future

W. A. Brogden and N. A. Lamb

Although the Denburn formed the western boundary of Aberdeen in the 18th century it is now central to the city and it appears that it has always played a more important role in the development of the city than its present, or its nature at the end of the 18th century would suggest. It is along the Denburn that the very earliest settlements of what was to become Aberdeen took place.

From Woolmanhill in the north where there is evidence of a very ancient settlement extending to the junction of the Denburn and the Dee to the South, perhaps the site of the Roman camp Devanah, and in the middle of the this lower stretch of the Denburn valley is the Green the beginning of Aberdeen's history. Of the likely contenders to be the source of name for the city neither Dee nor Don fits linguistically nor topographically whereas the Den answers both and is very likely to be the source of the name Aberdeen. Indeed from the 12th century onwards Aberden is often the preferred spelling.

Therefore it is not to our surprise that such a topographically and historically important site will occupy a central place in the development of the town. Indeed it has done – as we have seen in Hamilton's gracefully handsome bridge at the entrance of the city. But even in that gesture is the notion of a problem overcome, and the Denburn as problem has preoccupied the citizens of Aberdeen at various times since then, and indeed it concerns us again today as we approach the millennium.

The impulse we have called Neo-Classical was about solving problems: such as those entry into towns through roads and waterways, pursuing new forms of building but employing the flexible language of classical architecture. As part of that impulse – and probably a most significant one – was the development of industry and trade and our earliest views of the Denburn show much evidence of those activities – the bleaching fields, and the smoke stacks south of the Green are most prominent. To the north was another industrial area, the artisan quarter of Gilcomston already

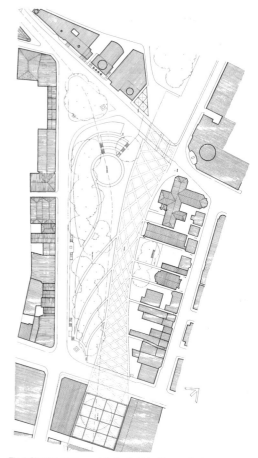

Fig. 2 *Site plan of proposed design for Union Terrace Gardens.* Drawing by N. A. Lamb

Previous page: Fig. 1 *Location of proposed design for Union Terrace Gardens within Aberdeen's urban fabric.* Drawing by N. A. Lamb

active in the 17th century. To that we may add was that the city was a building site for 40 years and although it was recognised as being Picturesque, it was messy, smoky and probably a smelly scene too.

The manifestation of trade and industry began to impinge on Union Bridge itself in the 1850s by which time the Neo-Classical suburbs on th west side of the Denburn had become a preferred dwelling place for citizens. A railway station was proposed for the south-west corner, and after much deliberation the railway line to the north was resited from Waterloo Quay to run beside the Denburn. The busy phase of development seems to have been overtaken in Aberdeen by a concern to beautify in the 1860s. The Denburn valley becomes the site of municipal gardens in a manner similar to that of Prince's Street Gardens in Edinburgh, at first exploiting the Corbie Haugh at the western end of the bridge but soon taking in the canalised Denburn itself and even a model sewage works. Within two decades the Union Terrace Gardens begin to achieve their current form.

Perhaps from this period also comes the perception that the backs of Belmont Street are less pleasing to look upon than the handsomer fronts of Union Terrace – especially as stables and other outbuildings encroached into the gardens behind Belmont Street and began to change into little industries along the Denburn Road. Although the north prospect begins to be perceived as untidy, and may not be august enough for a town now playing an active part in the Empire. The north end of Union Terrace Gardens is formed into an earth bank again similarly to the Mound in Edinburgh, but in the case of Aberdeen it was purposely made to mask the view of the untidy Gilcomston and it became a site for the new Library, parish church and ultimately the principal Theatre.

This was part of the new project begun just as Union Street was completed – the last house was built in the 1870s. Abercrombie had called for two major streets running parallel, and forming a

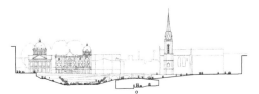

Fig. 3 *Section through the proposed design for Union Terrace Gardens looking north.* Drawing by N. A. Lamb

somewhat regular grid. What he refered to as School-Hill Street, becomes the Picturesque link between Rosemount and Broad Street. The new scheme was to make a new curving street from Broad Street to the suburbs by Rosemount. This was to be done by 'improving' Upperkirkgate and Schoolhill, bridging over the Denburn, twice, embanking the Gardens and joining Mount Street at Rosemount Viaduct. There were socially laudable reasons for this project – the clearance of the slums at Broad Street and Upperkirkgate end, but it was mostly a way of connecting the city centre with one of its most agreeable suburbs and at the same time masking the squalid industry and tumbledown neighbourhoods.

It was an early exercise in Sitte-an planning – both Picturesque and medieval and a repudiation of the grid as universal pattern. It was as significant as the Union Street project: indeed, perhaps we should view both as neo-classical schemes – the Union Street project clearly 'rational', the Rosemount scheme 'romantic', since these two notions were always present in the Neo-Classical period.

With this embankment between Schoolhill and Rosemount Viaduct the north end of the Denburn Gardens was handsomely finished, as was the west side, largely re-built in the early 20th century in a grander institutional form. The southern part of the valley remained unblushingly industrial with factories, the Joint Station, railway and harbour lands and the trawl fishing suburb of Torry in full view. In the second quarter of the 20th century designers and planners addressed this problem. In the Dobson Chapman report *The Granite City* of 1949 the south end is built over, and all industrial untidiness was to disappear. In the mid-1960s the southern end of the valley was masked in the coarsest way possible – a great ugly girder bridge was built to carry a row of shops – if ever a planning blunder cried out for restitution this is it. Later still the Trinity shopping centre was built over the valley, and now we have a newly constructed expressway running through the valley.

Fig. 4 *View south from Union Terrace Gardens towards Simpson's Gloucester Hotel and Union Bridge.* Drawing by N. A. Lamb

A problem had been identified and a class of solutions to answer it were being formulated – the answer – build over it . A number of schemes have come from the Scott Sutherland School of Architecture, Robert Gordon University, addressing the Denburn from as early as 1944. One from James Galletly's civic design studio of 1954 by Ian Imlach shows a park-like garden covering not only the untidy Denburn Road but the railway as well.

At the end of the 20th century – perhaps continuing what may become a tradition – Aberdeen feels it must make a bold gesture of urban improvement, and a scheme has been developed which would raise the garden up to the level of Union Bridge, build at a higher level in much of Belmont Street's backlands, and cover the road with parking garages and commercial opportunities. We have modeled that proposal electronically, and its merits are plain for anyone to see.

That design comes about because of the perception that the Denburn Valley is problematic and also is presupposed to require a 'commercial' or developer's solution to be 'viable'. But suppose we isolate the few real problems that the gardens have and attempt to resolve them in as simple a way as possible – as a civic gesture, perhaps in a similar manner to those imaginatively conceived proposals for King and Union Street. Firstly, what are the real problems? It is presently impossible to approach Union Bridge as the Lord Provost and his officials did when they opened it, that is from Schoolhill. Nor is it possible to proceed from the statue of King Edward to Schoolhill. In consequence the gardens are sequestrated and lovely in themselves, but being in a sense 'a dead end' they do not engender a sense of security.

The other real problem is Union Bridge itself and especially the way its south side has been treated. Any solution which addressed these issues might have the chance of success and retain the character of the Denburn Valley – that is a garden in a valley, with at least the metaphor of a river surrounded by remarkably handsome buildings at high level – the Library, His Majesty's Theatre. St Marks, the Art Gallery, the Triple Kirks (we earnestly hope to be restored), the new Cinegraphic Institute, the Congregational Church, the old terminal blocks of Union Street, Simpson's Hotel, Smith's Old Trinity Hall – C&A's and the grand sweep of Union Terrace itself.

It must be very clearly re-stated that the Union Terrace Gardens is an urban park in the heart of the city not a piece of leftover ground ripe for exploitation. It is not as accessible as most would wish it to be and the now crowded and obscured Union Bridge presents only a shadow of its former glory and the architectural merit of Belmont Street is largely unappreciated, whereas that of Union Terrace and Rosemount Viaduct are insufficiently celebrated. If a means could be found to bring right these imperfections Union Terrace Gardens would begin to play a uniting and regenerating role in the heart of the city. We have thought about these problems and as a University School of Architecture and the Architectural Heritage Society, we hold a brief or no special interest apart from the City of Aberdeen itself.

The roadway and railway we would cover by a simple but elegant terrace which is to be made up of a series of walkways connecting the two sides diagonally, bridging the gap and recreating a metaphorical river Denburn. Between the primary structural elements are coloured cast glass sections which reinforce the effect but at the same time can also be easily walked upon. They allow light into the road and rail level below and at night time the reverse occurs as lights from the traffic below can be seen from above, animating the metaphorical river. These sections will also take planters for flowers in summer and a variety of other celebrational decorations at other times of the year. Additional more powerful lights would be turned on at special times to light the gardens from below allowing the terrace to bring light into the gardens. Seen from above this could produce a spectacular effect giving substance to the re-found historic urban park.

Fig. 5 *Section through proposed design for Union Terrace Gardens looking south towards Union Bridge. Drawing by N. A. Lamb*

What we propose is a partly terraced, partly sculptured, multi-coloured, multi-functional place of culture, the genuine heart of the city which will adapt with seasonal variations from on one hand a typically magnificent floral display in summer to an outdoor skating arena in winter.

The other real problem with Union Terrace Gardens is Union Bridge Itself. The south side is crudely masked by the row of shops from the 1960s, these we propose to remove. This will liberate the south-west terminal block of the original Union Street (The Trinity Hall) and re-unite it with Simpson's matching sentinel on the northern side of the street. The Neo-Classical gateway to the medieval city would be reinstated as once again we would appreciate Hamilton's Union Bridge and its entry buildings. This will give Union Bridge space to 'breathe' and mark its presence on both the south side as well as the gardens to the north. The Trinity Shopping Centre's rough edge thus exposed will be remodeled and reunited to the street by means of an all-year-round civic space; a city square shared between the city and the shopping centre. Glazed in the simplest manner possible such a pavilion in the right hands would be a celebration in itself creating a winter garden that would unite street and terrace levels allowing access to Union Terrace Gardens by way of the arch of Union Bridge. To the south links would be established It to the railway, the bus station, the parking garage and the ancient Green. Thus could be created a 21st-century city gateway at Union Bridge and Union Street reinforcing its historical importance. The trees and parkland of the gardens would be restored and the access to the gardens greatly improved by way of a series of new ramps which will allow disabled access throughout. It would be possible to traverse the gardens, safely and easily from Union Terrace to Belmont Street and Union Street to the Art Gallery, Library or His Majesty's Theatre. As part of such proposals the arches under Union Terrace could be used more positively; perhaps as an extension to business or Caledonian Hotel as bars and cafés at garden level encouraging lively usage of the gardens at every hour. Even if they were left as they are at present, the greater number of people passing would ensure a happier usage. At the north end we suggest another glass pavilion east of his Majesty's Theatre, which could act as both a new foyer to the theatre and provide a studio theatre space below. Not only would it echo the glass pavilion at Union Bridge but also act as a pivot for future development north of Union Terrace Gardens.

The bold decisions that created Union Street and King Street 200 years ago were taken by a city that intended a lasting legacy for its future citizens and indeed today we can look back and celebrate the vision which helped Aberdeen attain its deserved position as one of the country's finest and most beautiful cities. With the coming millennium and the bicentennial of the street the city has again seen the opportunity to commission ideas for a similar visionary gesture. We hope most earnestly that the lessons from the past are heard, and guide the selection of proposals that will have no other interest but that of the City of Aberdeen itself.

Below: Fig. 6 *Long section through proposed design for Union Terrace Gardens.* Drawing by N. A. Lamb

Right: Fig. 7 *View north from Union Bridge towards His Majesty's Theatre, St Marks, and the Library.* Drawing by N. A. Lamb

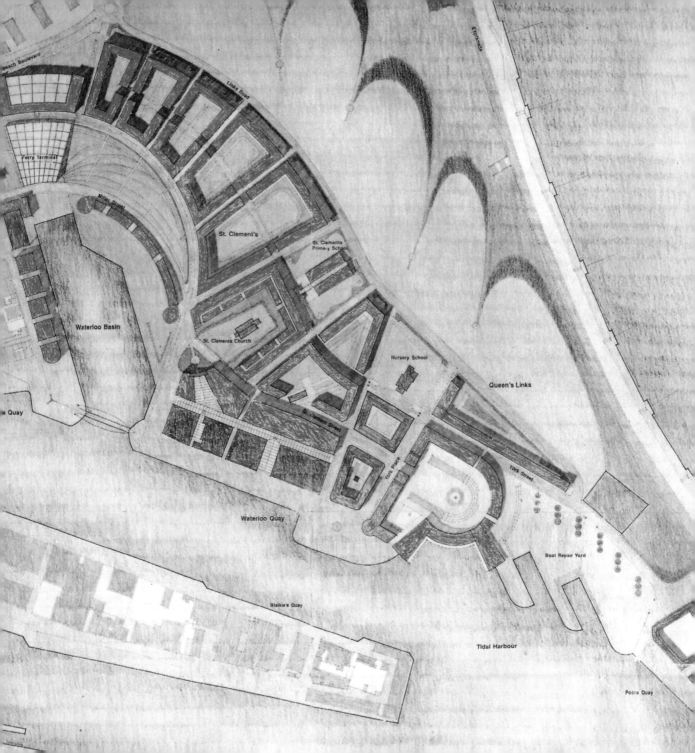

Ferry Terminal

Links Road

St. Clement's

St. Clements Primary School

Miller Street

Waterloo Basin

St. Clements Church

Nursery School

Queen's Links

St. Clement Street

York Place

York Street

Waterloo Quay

Boat Repair Yard

Blaikie's Quay

Tidal Harbour

Pocra Quay

Esplanade

Respecting the Town:
The Office of Urban Architecture
B. M. Evans

Scotland has a proud and distinct urban tradition. The medieval Scots burgh with its long linear high street and characteristic 'fish bone' pattern of rigs forms the basis of many fine towns. Those which grew into the cities of Scotland had this medieval form augmented or replaced with the rational ideas of Georgian planning and the ornament of the Victorians. In the set-piece civic grandeur of Edinburgh or the driving enterprise of Glasgow's new towns, fine, coherent townscapes were created as vibrant places for Scottish society and enterprise. At the close of the 20th century, however, there are few contemporary examples of quality urban design to add to this legacy from previous centuries. This paper considers the legacy of land-use planning and its influences on urban design in Scotland. Current trends and the rediscovery of urban design values in the planning process are examined by reference to a number of recent projects. Finally, the Scottish case is considered in the context of European experience illustrated by examples from Barcelona and Turin.

The benefits of the planning system are many and diverse, but as it has evolved, the philosophy and practice of planning has created a four-fold legacy for urban design which has influenced the way we think about our towns and cities and, as a consequence, upon their form. First, planning legislation was developed, not in response to fine townscapes, but in response to the problems, particularly health, of urbanisation in the 19th century when a large-scale population shift and urban expansion created new challenges for British cities. A system of housing, health, community and labour relations was evolved as a framework for urban management. From the 1820s onward, increased intervention and regulation of community affairs developed as part of United Kingdom democracy. This led to ordered working hours, conditions of work, and provision of water supply, sewage, fuel, light, education, welfare and health. Thus British cities became watered, drained, sewered, lit and paved. Houses and buildings were regulated to provide the basis of an efficient and healthy way of urban life. In this context, planning developed as an activity of urban government in a trend towards

Previous page: Fig. 1 *St.Clements Masterplan, Aberdeen.* OUA 1992/93

comprehensive city regulation. By the 20th century, municipal control and public direction over urban and community affairs was well-established and largely respected.[1]

1. G. E. Cherry, *The Evolution of British Town Planning*, Leonard Hill, 1974, pp. 6-7.

Fig. 2: *Engraving of New Lanark.* The Pilgrim Press Ltd.

2. G. E. Cherry, *op. cit.*, pp. 17-23.

Second, there is a long-established principle to resolve urban problems by relocation, usually to a greenfield site. The process began with the building of villages for workers by wealthy manufacturers, often in rural areas, with good housing and community facilities. The best were exemplary, well laid out, spacious and embodied the social idealism of the time. In 1784, Robert Owen created New Lanark around the cotton mills at the Falls of Clyde as a manufacturing village to implement his ideas of social reform. A benevolent entrepreneur, Owen aimed to create a community free from ignorance, vice and disease – a manufacturing settlement of good houses with a range of community facilities. Over 100 years later, the 19th century ended with similar experiments by the Lever Brothers in Port Sunlight and the Cadbury family at Bournville.[2]

In turn, the Garden-City movement had its roots in the experiments of the 19th century. The idea of combating urban and housing problems – particularly the consequences of growth – with new communities and settlements was very popular. In 1898, Ebenezer Howard published *Tomorrow – a Peaceful Path to Real Reform* which was retitled *Garden Cities of Tomorrow* in 1902. Howard was concerned that people would continue to migrate into overcrowded cities and he proposed new satellite towns of 30,000, self-supporting with a green belt separating them from existing cities. Howard's ideas led first to the formation of a *Garden City Association* and then to the establishment of a company to build a prototype. Howard's ideas covered land ownership, manufacturing, sanitary conditions and the scientific development of towns. In 1907, the Garden City Association was renamed the Garden City and Town Planning Movement.[3]

3. F. Schaffer, *The New Town Story*, Paladin 1972, pp 19-25.

Supported by the Cadbury and Lever families, the early examples such as Hampstead Garden suburb led to the first round of new towns such as Letchworth and Welwyn Garden City and eventually to the Scottish new towns of Cumbernauld, East Kilbride, Irvine, Glenrothes and Livingston, and the remarkable city of Milton Keynes. The concept of a new greenfield settlement was conceived of at New Lanark. In the United Kingdom, the development of the concept through the Garden City and the New Town movements took place almost exclusively in England and was re-imported into Scotland in the decades following the Second World War. It continues today in proposals for new settlements.

Pre-occupation with these ideas and a concern for the appropriate use of land and distribution of resources flourished during the creative tensions of the Second World War and generated three remarkable state papers. The first, the Royal Commission on the Distribution of Industrial Population under Sir Montague Barlow led to the impetus for overspill and new town movements. The second, the Expert Committee on Compensation and Betterment under Mr Justice Uthwatt considered compulsory purchase and compensation in an endeavour to lay the foundations for the reconstruction of post-war Britain. The third, the Expert Committee on Land Utilisation in Rural Areas under the chairmanship of Lord Justice Scott was concerned with the well-being of rural communities, the maintenance of agriculture and with factors affecting the location of industry.[4] These pieces of work laid the foundation for the environmental 'magnum opus' of the first post-war labour government (the 1947 Town and Country Planning Act) which established a mechanism to implement the vision of the nation's planning.

4. G. E. Cherry, *op. cit.*, pp. 120-122.

A third influence developed as these ambitious programmes were being implemented in the post-war years and faith in technology became paramount. Planning thought imported technological concepts such as systems theory. Inevitably, advances of this nature were made at the centre of the technological revolution in the United States and, along with the intellectual ideas, the UK imported some of the value systems and perceptions of distance and space from a sparsely populated pioneer country to the ancient,

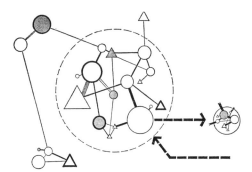

Fig. 3 *System diagram*. J. Brian McLoughlin

5. J. B. McLoughlin, *Urban & Regional Planning : A Systems Approach*, Faber & Faber, London, 1970.

6. Department of the Environment, *A Development Plan Manual*, HMSO, 1970.

7. Department of the Environment, *op. cit.*, p . 105.

'Planning authorities should recognise that aesthetics is an extremely subjective matter. They should not therefore impose their tastes on developers simply because they believe them to be superior. Developers should not be compelled to conform to the fashion of the moment at the expense of the individuality, originality or traditional styles. Nor should they be asked to adapt designs which are unpopular with their customers or clients.'

8. R.K. Home, *Deregulating UK Planning Control in the 1980s*, Cities, Nov. 1991, pp. 292-300.

9. Department of the Environment, *Aesthetic Control*, Circular 2/1985.

multi-layered and densely populated islands of the United Kingdom with its European landscape and urban structures.

Ideas developed by Brian McLoughlin[5] and others became enshrined in official publications such as the Development Plan Manual[6]. This work made many valuable contributions to town and country planning – including the principles for organising regional planning in a system of structure plans. However, applied indiscriminately, these techniques reduce the planning process to a set of formulae which can be applied irrespective of the nature of place. This is evidenced by the examples quoted in the Development Plan Manual for the fictional county of *Planshire*.[7] The manual's method for dealing with town centres demonstrates the failure of this approach which ignores rather than rejects the genius of place which, along with a sense of community, is one of the key issues determining the vitality, quality and success of the city and town centre. The principles expressed in the Development Plan Manual were enshrined in government circulars in Scotland as well as England and Wales. These documents together with predicted traffic growth and the enthusiasm for highway engineering and transportation planning led to many of the excesses visited upon our towns and cities in the 1960s and 1970s.

Fourth, the government elected in 1979 introduced a policy of 'disengagement' to remove intervention from the processes of planning and development. The technological approach was replaced with one where administrative efficiency and minimum intervention became the key indices by which the effectiveness of planning was to be monitored.[8] Concern for design, aesthetics and the genius of place became even more invisible.[9]

All the forces described above influenced urban design throughout the United Kingdom. However, the differences between the planning systems are apparent, and statements as strong as that quoted opposite did not find their way into contemporary circulars published by the Scottish Office. In the last five years, recent initiatives have recognised that skill and experience, good design and concern for place are fundamental tenets to careful urban

10. Scottish Office, *Town Centre Management*, Planning Advice Note PAN35, 1989. Refer also to: Dept of the Environment, Urban & Economic Development Group, *Vital & Viable Town Centres: Meeting the Challenge*, HMSO, 1994 ; Department of the Environment, *Quality in Town and Country, A Discussion Document*, 1994; Shaw,M. (ed), *Caring for Our Towns and Cities*, The Civic Trust and Boots the Chemist, 1993.

11. Scottish Enterprise, *The Network Strategy*, 1994, p. 9.

12. Gillespies, *Glasgow City Centre Public Realm: Strategy and Guidelines*, Strathclyde Regional Council, 1995.

13. Gillespies, *op. cit.*, p. 39.

14. Strathclyde Regional Council, *Glasgow City Centre Millennium Plan, Transport Strategy Consultation Brochure*, 1995.

Left: Fig 4 *The regular grid and characteristic plan of central Glasgow.* National Remote Sensing Centre

design and city regeneration. These issues have become central to the debate and now exercise the minds of ministers. In Scotland, the sustained programme of urban renewal in the 1970s and 1980s and the distinctiveness of the Scottish planning system gave an early impetus to careful urban regeneration and the re-examination of urban-design issues. For example, a planning advice note on town-centre management was produced approximately five years in advance of a similar document in England and Wales.[10] The economic importance of these shifts in policy is underlined by the concept of 'place-competitiveness' contained in the network strategy of Scottish Enterprise.[11]

The examples described below examine ways in which changing attitudes encourage the appropriate attention and respect to be paid to the important legacy of urban design in Scotland.

In 1995, a strategy for the public realm of Glasgow City Centre was published by Strathclyde Regional Council, Glasgow City Council and the Glasgow Development Agency.[12] Prepared by Gillespies, the strategy defines the public realm as the space outside – the streets, spaces and lanes which make up the cohesive pleasant, safe and exciting matrix of a great city – providing the setting for grand buildings, the thoroughfares of commerce and the spaces for activity, street theatre, contemplation and promenading.[13] The aim of the work is to provide guidance on how to take advantage of the environmental and urban-design opportunities which will be created by the ambitious millennium plan for traffic management in the city centre being promoted by the regional council.[14]

The work is set in the context of Glasgow's continuing urban regeneration which has set wide-ranging aims for the city centre which include: commitment to economic health and vibrancy; the quality of the environment as a whole; and the enhancement of people's comfort and convenience. In recent years, there has been a noticeable improvement in the appearance of Glasgow's buildings, but the quality of public spaces has lagged far behind. Many proposals for the improvement of the public realm have been prepared but these are mostly fragmented and together do not constitute a coherent design strategy.

The strategy recognises the importance of the inherent character and inherited townscape of Glasgow and seeks to explain the public realm through an understanding of the city's urban plan, topography and built form with particular emphasis on the regular grid, the shape of the ground formed by glaciation and the form and proportion of the city's streets. This analysis is complemented with a consideration of the way in which people use and perceive the city centre, by examining the distribution of institutions, public buildings, key pedestrian movement, open spaces and the nature of city-centre neighbourhoods. Finally, the consequences of transportation are considered for the essential purposes of moving people around the city and for servicing its needs.

The strategy for the public realm stops short of an overall urban design strategy for Glasgow City Centre which embraces the form, proportion and cohesion of buildings. However the strategy recognises that the inherited townscape of the city centre – a regular grid of streets laid over a rolling topography – brings order and consistency to the urban structure and a 'sense of place' to the city centre. The strategy calls for the retention of the cohesive matrix of streets and spaces as a fundamental issue in considering improvements to the public realm.

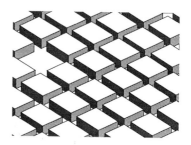

An ordering principle of streets and spaces is proposed with a hierarchy based on: the historical and architectural significance of urban form; the presence of institutions, attractions and venues; and the importance of retailing, offices, pedestrian routes and vehicle thoroughfares. The hierarchy consists of three elements: principal streets and spaces of architectural value, cultural or historical importance and overwhelming use; a matrix of robust urban streets which give definition to the city form of urban centre; opportunities to enhance the quality of spaces and the settings to major buildings

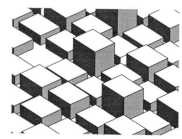

Fig. 5 *Considering the Town Plan*. A regular grid laid over undulating topography. The configuration of the original blocks have had their massing altered over time. The regular grid remains. Strategy for the Public Realm in Glasgow, Strathclyde Regional Council

Principal
Streets & Spaces
•
*settings for key
attractions/institutions/facilities*
•
*settings for premier pieces
of architecture*
•
*spaces and streets representing
the heart of the City Centre*
•
*places heavily frequented
by residents, visitors and
influential persons*

Major
Streets & Spaces
•
*settings for important
attractions/institutions/facilities*
•
areas of notable architectural quality
•
significant streets and spaces

Minor
Streets & Spaces
•
other streets and spaces

Fig. 6 *An Ordering Principle for Streets and Spaces in Central Glasgow*,
Gillespies

15. Gillespies, *op. cit.*, pp. 36-38.

and institutions; and, a network of public streets and spaces which support these more important functions and uses. Although of less civic importance their coherence is vital to the legibility and form of central Glasgow[15]. In this way, a balanced view of the importance of streets and spaces was developed based upon the significance of the urban form. Within the strategy, design guidelines have been developed for management and maintenance; hard and soft landscape; street furniture; signing and lighting; and other important issues such as public art and the amelioration of Glasgow's wet and windy climate. The guidelines endeavour to deal explicitly with the subtle vocabulary of the city's streets which goes largely unnoticed but contributes to the overall cohesion of townscape and streetscape. When handled insensitively these elements disrupt both the rhythm and the composition of the street. For example, considerable attention is given to the appropriate design of and material for kerbs which can subtly reinforce building disposition but are too often coarsely manipulated in the interests of traffic calming to the detriment of the legibility of the street.

The analysis and design guidelines of the strategy for the public realm are being used to inform the detailed design of a number of high-quality demonstration projects at Candleriggs, Royal Exchange Square, Buchanan Street and Hope Street. This work represents a major step towards the future conservation and sensitive development of the notable town plans of Scottish towns and cities.

A parallel initiative promoted by the Glasgow Development Agency, the Crown Street Regeneration Project in Glasgow will result in the comprehensive urban regeneration of approximately 40 acres of the Gorbals neighbourhood in the inner city located immediately to the south of the River Clyde. The original Gorbals village was developed as a middle-class suburb in the early 19th century but became a notorious slum at the end of the 19th and early part of the 20th centuries. Comprehensively redeveloped in the 1960s, the quality of building did not live up to the aims of the Modernist principles which set out its ambitious high-rise masterplan. The image and reality of slum living was not conquered and the fierce community spirit was severely challenged. But by the late 1980s the city was again ready to face the challenge of regenerating the area.

Comprehensive regeneration has been attempted before in Glasgow notably in the Glasgow Eastern Area Renewal (GEAR) Project carried out in the late 1970s and early 1980s by the former Scottish Development Agency.[16] However, the organisers of the Crown Street project have taken great care to involve the local community in the renewal efforts and explicit references are made to the urban plan and built form of Glasgow in developing urban-design principles for the project. The masterplan has developed from the competition winning submission by Campbell Zogolovitch Wilkinson and Gough and interprets the traditional elements of grid, street, block and tenement to provide context for a balanced community and modern urban living.[17] The project area is rectangular and orientated on a north-south axis. The masterplan creates a development of nine urban blocks using the four-storey tenements as the basic building element. The project aims to reconcile the highest standards of design and quality with realistic assumptions about the development market and the availability of public-sector funding.

The legacy of fine urban design in Scotland is threatened not only in town and city centre. Poor and functionally derived extensions to towns can prejudice the integrity and cohesion of town centres. 'Fitting New Housing Development into the Landscape' (PAN 44)[19] deals with expansion at the town edge and is part of a series of advice and guidance notes published by Scottish Office which emphasises the importance of design in the planning process. PAN44 develops the theme of sustainable design from earlier Government advice including 'This Common Inheritance' [20] and is consistent with the policies and advice produced by other public agencies in Scotland, including Scottish Natural Heritage, as well as public bodies elsewhere in the UK.

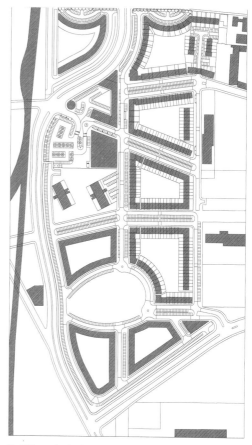

Fig. 7 *Masterplan for Crown Street*, Crown Street Regeneration Project

16. D. Draffan and R. Leclerc, *The Glasgow Eastern Area Renewal Project*, Town Planning Review, Vol. 55, No. 3, July 1984, pp. 335-351.

17. Crown Street Regeneration Project, *Masterplan Report*, Glasgow Development Agency, 1990, pp. 9-12 & p. 31.

18. Scottish Office Environment Department, *Town Centre Management, Planning Advice Note PAN 35*, The Scottish Office, 1989.

19. Scottish Office Environment Department, *Fitting New Housing Development into the Landscape*, Planning Advice Note PAN 44, The Scottish Office, 1994.

The design manual from PAN 44 was prepared for the Scottish Office Environment Department by Gillespies and develops the work of the former Countryside Commission for Scotland, published as *Tomorrow's Architectural Heritage*[21], and the practice's ongoing participation in the planning and design of a number of new and expanded settlements throughout the United Kingdom.

Scotland has a proud tradition of new and expanded settlement planning. Many 18th- and 19th-century planned villages and small towns have matured to offer a high quality of life for the residents as well as becoming an essential part of the country's architectural and cultural heritage. In many instances this tradition persisted through the inter-war and immediate post-war years. However, the experience of the last few decades indicates an urgent need to create new places of distinction, of the late 20th century, but with the prospect of becoming the heritage of future generations. PAN 44 encourages all those involved in development to become familiar with and learn from the legacy of planned towns and cities.

For the reasons outlined in the initial part of this paper, design issues are often addressed too late in the development process. Unless the objectives for a project and the standards of design and development to be achieved are understood and appreciated at the outset it will be difficult, if not impossible, to achieve the quality required at a later stage. Issues of quality need to be treated as important considerations at the outset in the designation of land and in site selection. Land values may have to reflect the design standards and environmental quality expected today and this may be possible if design requirements are established before land is purchased.

PAN 44 recommends a rigorous and disciplined approach to the study of the site and the development programme. Particular emphasis is placed on examination of the site, its topography, climate and the landscape character with a view to establishing capacity for development. It is important to enhance

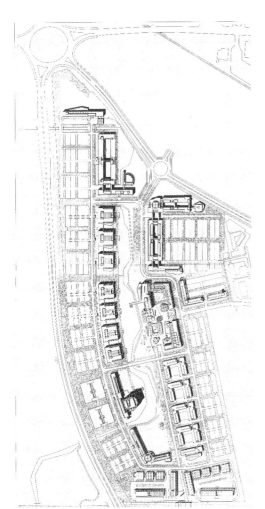

Fig. 8 *Masterplan for Maybury Business Park*, Richard Meier & Partners and Edinburgh Enterprise

20. Department of the Environment, *This Common Inheritance, Britain's Environmental Strategy*, Cm 1200, HMSO, 1990.

21. B. M. Evans, J. M. Fladmark and G.Y. Mulvagh, *Tomorrow's Architectural Heritage: Landscape & Buildings in the Countryside*, Mainstream, Edinburgh, 1991.

latent as well as obvious characteristics of place.[22] Analysis will not create the quality of plan nor the quality of place that is required for the future. The creative design process carried out by personnel with skill and experience is an essential part of this process. The design principles in the document illustrate how various studies into landscape form, building shape, plot size, road and parking configurations can be applied and through a process of synthesis, conceptual design and checking the requirements of the brief, an elegant and appropriate solution can be evolved.

This process of analysis and design is not intended to be a blueprint. The weight applied to each of the factors will vary with particular circumstances. Rather it is the rigour with which the process is applied which is emphasised in the advice note. There is clearly a need to consider these issues in the preparation of development plans at all scales if design is to be treated seriously. If new or expanded settlements are to be given the importance which historical examples suggest, then the skills of site planning and design synthesis will have to be re-learned by all those involved in the process.

Richard Meier's masterplan for the business park to the west of Edinburgh predates the publication of Planning Advice Note PAN 44 but clearly exhibits many of the principles advocated by it. Brian Edwards has identified four general principles in Meier's work which are exhibited in the masterplan for the Maybury Business Park: local references should be identified, considered and reinterpreted; geometric order underpins design; structure should be modified by consideration of space and time; and rotational or volumetric shifts enhance design.[23] At Maybury, Meier's vocabulary of abstract modern design is tempered by respect for context in a modern interpretation of the principles of order and spatial structure evident in Edinburgh's New Town – in particular, the relationship between urban blocks and landscaped gardens and the unifying effect of streets visually and as a datum for development. The extent of the Maybury Business Park Plan (140 acres) is approximately the same

ANALYSIS CHECKLIST

✓ Ascertain Land Ownership in and Around Site

✓ Refer to Local Plan

✓ Examine Landform, Slope and Contours

✓ Undertake Landscape Analysis

✓ Define Landscape Character

✓ Undertake Visual Assessment

✓ Make Photographic Record

✓ Compile Climatic Information

✓ Identify Vegetation around Site

✓ Establish Ground and Subsoil Conditions

✓ Refer to Existing Services Information

✓ Confirm Developers Requirements

DESIGN CHECKLIST

✓ Establish Landscape Capacity

✓ Define Development Concept

✓ Determine Scale and Density of Development

✓ Establish Structure and Layout

✓ Determine Height and Massing

✓ Develop Planting Framework

✓ Integrate Access and Parking Requirements

✓ Consider Orientation Implications

✓ Compile House Types and Plot Studies

✓ Develop Sketch Layouts

✓ Ongoing Testing of Proposals by Brief and Consultations

✓ Prepare Masterplans

Fig. 9 *Analysis and design checklist from PAN 44*, Scottish Office

22. Scottish Office Environment Dept, *op. cit.*, 1994, pp. 14-16.

23. B. Edwards, *Meier's Maybury Masterplan*, RIBA Journal, Sept. 1989, pp. 46-47.

24. Richard Meier & Partners, *Maybury Business Technology Park: The Overall Plan*, Enterprise Edinburgh, 1989, Planning and Architectural Philosophy Statement.

as one of the later phases of the New Town and the rhythm, pattern and size of urban blocks is also broadly compatible. Meier has acknowledged his references to James Craig's masterplan for the Edinburgh New Town and the distinction between large corporate buildings of up to 14 storeys and the smaller regular and repeated four-storey office blocks reflects the distinction of churches and housing in Craig's plan.[24]

Both Maybury at the edge of Edinburgh and Crown Street in the centre of Glasgow prefer urban compactness to suburban sprawl, with site planning exhibiting compact urban blocks, well-defined streets and legible townscape. These plans clearly exhibit the evidence of changing attitudes to urban design, the rediscovery of design values in the planning process and the hope of reinvigorating the Scottish contribution to urban design.

One of the most significant factors reflecting the way our society approaches towns and cities is the manner in which young professionals in Britain are trained to deal with the issues and develop the necessary skills. For decades young architects have been encouraged to conceive Modernist solutions to buildings with an emphasis on technology and on making an aesthetic statement rather than carefully fitting a modern solution within an appreciation of context, an approach which their professional forefathers carried through into urban planning in the post-war years. Later, young planners were recruited for their grasp of social-scientific matters resulting in a profession skilled in analysis but ignorant of design.

The Office of Urban Architecture (OUA) was conceived to help fill this gap by encouraging architects to think holistically about the city and to prepare their contributions accordingly. The OUA is a teaching and research initiative within the Scott Sutherland School of Architecture at the Robert Gordon University in Aberdeen and is one of a number of options which graduate architects elect to pursue in their final year at architecture school.

The teaching is studio-based and the group is organised as a formal design office. The students work both as a team and individually to communally assigned tasks. The process reveals the importance of team building, structured decision making, regular progress meetings, accurate recording of information, the need to reach consensus on the evolution of design concepts and working within a formalised project programme.

The students learn for themselves the importance of polished professional practice which assists with achieving the programme requirements of the OUA. Conventionally, professional practice training is, all too frequently, an unexciting necessity for architectural students in the completion of their course. It is a very significant part of the education of architects but often deals solely with matters such as professional indemnity insurance and contract law. One of the objectives of the OUA is to bring to senior student life the realisation that high-quality professional practice is not a adjunct to, but an essential part of, the practice of design.

An exercise like the OUA establishes its own momentum but the point of departure is as important as the point of arrival. The theme for the work is guided by the tutors to help ensure with some degree of certainty that the students will encounter a number of current and pertinent issues in their odyssey of self-discovery. The skill in selecting a theme is to achieve a balance between the obvious and the obscure. The emphasis lies in revealing that rational thought and the application of design to strategic decision making can help to reinforce the coherence of the city and set a meaningful brief within which to carry out detailed design.

Fig. 10 *Exploring an Urban Village for St. Clements, Aberdeen*, Scott MacKenzie, OUA 1992/93

The process starts with the selection of an appropriate neighbourhood for study. A detailed study of context is accompanied by a review of theory and practice and an examination of relevant comparators. The aim is to establish principles for intervention and a formal masterplan which combines a thorough study of functional elements such as climate, topography, accessibility, together with philosophical elements underpinning structure, form and hierarchy. In particular, the students are encouraged to consider the public realm of street and spaces and the form and cohesiveness of the city before identifying, by consensus, the content of individual briefs for buildings and spaces.

An example of the themes explored is the urban villages initiative supported by the Prince of Wales.[25] Urban villages raise an exciting and wholly sustainable proposition, particularly if the concept can be realised by recycling degraded or underused urban land within existing urban areas.

25. T. Aldous, *Urban Villages: A Concept for Creating Mixed-Use Urban Developments on a Sustainable Scale*, Urban Villages Group, 1992.

This concept was researched by the OUA to test if a sizeable proportion of housing-need identified in the Grampian Structure Plan could be met in a mixed-use urban community within Aberdeen in an area known as St. Clements – lying between the city, the sea and the harbour. The proposition and masterplan developed by the students was subsequently tested in a series of individual architectural design projects within the context of the planned intervention.[26] The work has, with the benefit of a professional validation, made a contribution to the debate in Aberdeen about the future of urban neighbourhoods within the city centre.

26. Scott Sutherland School of Architecture & Gillespies, *St. Clements, Aberdeen, A Proposal to Recreate a City Centre Neighbourhood*, unpublished report of research, 1995.

The OUA has been running for four academic years and has established within the school of architecture, a programme of inquiry and design suitable for final-year architecture students. It is intended to continue and develop this model for inquiry and debate in future years.

The professional and educational examples described above are all initiatives directed to recovering urban design values in the planning process and offer encouragement for the future, but the extent to which this process needs continuing encouragement, investment and support can be seen when European examples are considered in comparison.

The European approach to the issues discussed in this paper is very informative. Post-war reconstruction has been concerned to a great degree with the recovery of national prestige and the rediscovery of cultural and design identities. Perhaps because of language, certainly because of culture, the functional separation of planning and architecture has never arisen to the same degree – the profession of urbanist is as well known as that of architect or lawyer. Nor has there been a predilection to leave urban problems unresolved through a process of relocation. In Europe the cultural importance of place is far too great.

In 1980, within the new policy for urban development established by the city authorities, Barcelona established a programme of transformation through major projects in strategic locations related to the most significant urban spaces. At the same time, it was decided to implement a programme of projects on a much larger scale which would employ the same methods and criteria but go beyond intervention at the local scale in individual neighbourhoods to assume a metropolitan stature and importance. Commitment to this approach was strengthened by winning the 1992 Olympic games.[27]

27. R. de Caceres and M. Ferrer, *Barcelona Espai Public*, Ajuntament de Barcelona, 1992.

The city authorities elected to locate the Olympic areas in parts of the city whose urban redevelopment would resolve a number of structural problems which had been apparent for some time and which would achieve strategic development objectives in linking different parts of the city. The four locations selected for the Olympic games were sited in areas lying between the orderly city of the 19th century and the relatively unplanned outer districts which had grown up as a result of demographic change and territorial expansion in the second half of the 20th century. These four areas form a cross whose arms symbolically mark the four cardinal points of the compass and indicate four extensions to Barcelona's process of reconstruction and development. They are now interlinked by new metropolitan traffic routes and connected to other outlying neighbourhoods which were previously isolated from each other and from the city.

Two of the areas – Montjüic Park and Poble Nou – are adjacent to the Mediterranean where the city has carried out a series of projects including the regeneration of the old port, restructuring the fishing settlement of Barcelonita and creating major new waterfront parades. Poble Nou, in a state of advanced industrial decay, was intended to become the next link in the extensive project which would open Barcelona to the sea with the creation of a new residential neighbourhood to be used in the first instance to accommodate athletes during the Olympic games.[28]

One of the characteristic features of recent urban design in Barcelona has been the reliance on the project rather than on formal land-use plans. The formal instrument regulating land use has not been abandoned but has been transformed in an attempt to introduce the positive elements which have emerged from international debate over the last decade concerning the operational functions of plan and project. This approach requires a clear definition of general aims and intentions and a conceptual scheme to clarify the lines of major decisions without being prescriptive about architectural and urban design matters. In effect, the result is a less figurative and less specific plan with regard to form and function, but one more related to the political and economic base of the city's future, leaving the formal definition and specifics of uses and urban structures to the project itself. [29]

The area chosen as the site of the Olympic village was an industrial zone of obsolete uses and structures which retained a number of dilapidated 19th-century factories. The area was severed from the city and the sea by two railway lines. The beaches had become a dumping ground for household rubbish and industrial waste, and the streets which followed the grid lines of the Cerda plan had lost their continuity and urban significance as a result of the severance. There was an accumulation of poorly balanced uses including a former fish market used as a car park, empty housing, a water treatment plant, low-value municipal warehouses, a prison, school buildings and heavy goods traffic chaotically superimposed on the area and using

28. Martorell, Bohigas, Mackay, Puigdomènech, *Barcelona 92, The Olympic Village*, Editorial Gustavo Gilli S.A., Barcelona, 1992, pp. 8-11.

Fig. 11 *Masterplan for the Olympic Village, Barcelona.* MBM Arquitectes, Barcelona

29. Martorell, Bohigas, Mackay, Puigdomènech, *op. cit.*

the seaside boulevard as an urban expressway. The area had become an urban void and represented an ideal space in which to carry out a thorough piece of urban regeneration establishing Barcelona's first modern seafront neighbourhood.[30]

30. Martorell, Bohigas, Mackay, Puigdomènech, *op. cit.*, pp . 14-26 and discussions with the authors in Barcelona, June 1993.

The success of Barcelona's Olympic village is well documented and is seen as a model for successful urban regeneration in Europe. It is not a panacea, however, and many lessons can be learned. For the purposes of this paper the positive lessons can be illustrated by two examples. First, the city of Barcelona was able to acquire the land from the state railway authority at existing use rather than market value. Partnerships were formed between the city and private developers for the creation of developments which were first leased for the duration of the Olympic games and later sold at market value. Based on the projected equity return, the city was able to advance-fund an enhanced specification for the public realm – notably the streets,spaces and parks.[31] A British city addressing these issues would face the challenge of negotiating with the land owner who would be concerned to maximise return to shareholders. Even if a British city is able to achieve such favourable conditions, the benefits are likely to be eliminated by a corresponding reduction in support from the treasury.

31. Martorell, Bohigas, Mackay, Puigdomènech, *op. cit.*

There are mechanisms to overcome this problem in the UK such as the establishment of a public-private sector venture company with a board made up of appropriate representatives. The Glasgow Garden Festival Company was a good example of the genre. But such initiatives take time, they require approvals and they are notorious for factionalism where time and effort are directed to the mechanism, not the product. In short they prevent communities acting decisively in pursuit of civic enterprise. City authorities are not perfect, but they remain an effective organisation to embrace and to promote a wider vision for the community, and it is to be hoped that the new unitary councils for Scottish cities will be able to grasp the opportunity for urban design leadership presented by this reorganisation with a minimum of government interference. Private enterprise can and will participate in this vision but cannot be expected to hold civic and community objectives as pre-eminent. By necessity these must be subservient to the requirements of business. The question of financial structures for development takes the urban debate into the political arena as evidenced by the inability to implement mechanisms in this country to address betterment and development-land value. The relevant provisions in the Town & Country Planning Act 1947 were never implemented and the ill-fated Community Land Act 1975 was short-lived.

The second example from Barcelona illustrates the insight, skill and experience which is necessary in architects and designers to account properly for civic and community objectives in their designs. It is normal in the design and management of major urban projects to divide the overall project into manageable parcels for the process of detailed design and construction. These packages are managed by design coordinators and project managers. Usually architects will work on a self-contained group of buildings such as an urban block selected as much for ease of construction management as for design and community objectives. In the case of the Olympic village in Barcelona, the sites were created around major intersections in the street thereby requiring considerable dialogue among design teams, with the community and with the various developers in order to develop a consensus.[32] This may not minimise the time taken to achieve a satisfactory design and realise the project, but it does demonstrate considerable maturity in understanding the forces of design expression and community cohesion which contribute so much to the forces which shape the city.

There are many contemporary programmes worthy of study in cities such as Berlin, Genoa, Oslo, Antwerp and Turin.[33] The final example considered here contrasts with the Barcelona case study and highlights the contribution to urban design which can be made by the official instrument of planning – the plan itself. Expressed in a beautifully drawn document, the third regulatory plan for the

32. Discussions June 1993, with David Mackay, MBM Arquitectes, responsible for the Olympic Village Masterplan and its subsequent design coordination.

33. J. Vanreusel, *Antwerp - Reshaping a City*, Blonde Artprinting International, Antwerp, 1990; P. Butenschon and T. Lindheim, *Det Nye Oslo : Ideer og Prosjekter for Bykjernen*, Dreyers Forlag A/S Oslo 1987; M. Mastropietro, *Colombo '92 : La Città, Il Porto, L'Esposizione*, Edizioni Lybra Immagine, Milan, 1992; M. Meijer, *Growth and Decline of European Cities: Changing Positions of Cities in Europe*, Urban Studies, Vol 30, No 6, 1993, pp. 981-990; K. Moe, *Tema med Variasjoner, Aker Brygge - Byggetrinn II*, Byggekunst no.7, 1989, pp. 510-524.

city of Turin has considered the future of the city as an exercise in strategic urban design. Recognising that most western European cities are reducing in population and – potentially – in area and density, the Turin plan has taken a strategic view of the future shape of the city concentrating on areas where compact development or land renewal will be required and where urban space and landscape can make a significant contribution to the future of the city. Within the detail of the plan, apparently detailed specifications of land use are revealed to be guidelines for the form, proportion and massing of buildings.[34] These guidelines, in fact, represent a loose framework which permits flexible and mixed use of buildings. Sadly, this strategic vision of the city would be difficult to achieve within the short-term, market-driven society of the United Kingdom.

Scotland enjoys a legacy of fine towns and cities. Over the last 200 years the urban form of Scotland has been reinforced by a series of elegant planned villages and city extensions.

Land-use planning has made an enormous contribution to the environment in Scotland but has had a major impact on urban design in the second half of the 20th century through an overriding concern for health, welfare and functional solutions; the resolution of intractable problems by relocation, usually to greenfield sites; the reduction of urban issues to a series of variables with solutions derived by the application of formulae; the exclusion of 'sense of place' from the formula; and the absence of clear top-down guidance expecting the market to provide development on a value-for-money, competitive and fast-track process. These forces have been evident in Scotland as elsewhere in the United Kingdom although the distinctive Scottish planning system has insulated urban design from some of the more extreme swings through a more consistent policy base.

Recently, there has been a sea-change in attitudes. A series of examples illustrate the recovery of urban design values in the planning process through: applications in practice designed to

Fig. 12 *Extract from Piano Regolatore di Torino*, Commune di Torino

34. Citta di Torino, *Piano Regolatore Generale di Torino*, Assessorato all'Urbanistica, Supplemento di "Torino Notizie" Rassegna del Commune a.XXV, marzo 1992.

conserve and enhance the inherited town plan; applications in practice to contribute sensitively to the extension of towns; and applications in education to broaden and enhance knowledge of the importance of inherited urban design. These examples represent positive initiatives but, as the review of some European examples indicates, there is still much work to do before today's practice can hope to create a heritage of the future which matches the legacy of the past.

ACKNOWLEDGEMENTS

I would like to record my thanks to Professor Robin Webster, Dr. Bill Brogden and Mr Neil Lamb of the Scott Sutherland School of Architecture, Robert Gordon University; my colleagues in Gillespies (particularly George Mulvagh, my partner and co-author of the PAN 44 Design Manual and 'Tomorrow's Architectural Heritage'); David Mackay of MBM Arquitectes, Barcelona; and Professor Donald Carruthers, Director, Strathclyde Roads. I would also like to acknowledge the many student members of the OUA who bring such enthusiastic enquiry to the challenges of urban design.

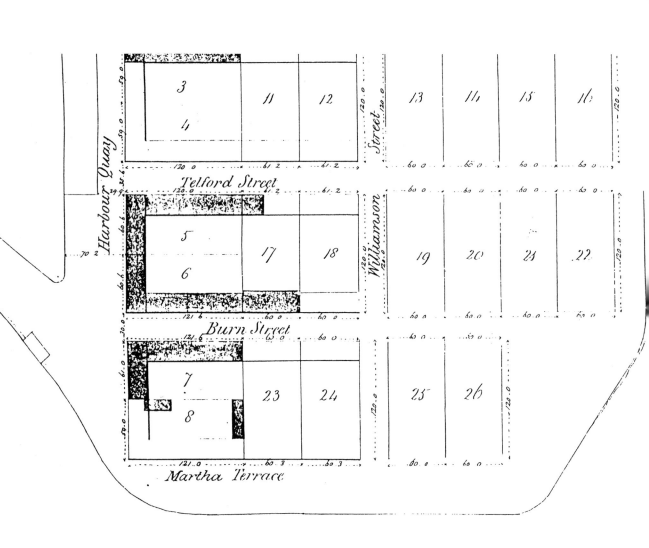

Teaching the Town: Lower Pulteneytown, Wick
John Donald

The British Fisheries Society was founded as a semi-charitable joint stock company in London in 1786 with the object of establishing fishing stations on the north or west coast of Scotland. It had a number of influential directors including Sir William Pulteney who recommended Thomas Telford to the society as professional adviser on the establishment of settlements and harbours. In 1790 Telford visited the west coast fishing stations which the society had already established, making suggestions for their improvement. He then journeyed along the Caithness coast in search of a site for a major harbour and fishing port. In this subsequent report to the society, Telford made a strong case for the improvement of the natural harbour at Wick to provide a major fishing station on land owned by Sir Benjamin Dunbar. The society did not act immediately, owing to other commitments, but on 11th March 1803 a contract was signed with Sir Benjamin in respect of 390 acres of land on the south side of the Wick River. This land included low-lying sandbanks at the mouth of the river and a large area of flat land above the steeply sloping bank to the south which contained excellent building stone suitable for quarrying. The first step was to raise money to build a harbour and Telford put the case to the treasury in May 1802. It was some three years before the money could be raised from the government, the Commissioners for Highland Roads and Bridges and local landowners. Telford was already employed on the design of bridges and harbours for the commissioners and in July 1805 he recommended George Burn, a local architect, to oversee the development of the new fishing station. The harbour was completed in 1813.

In parallel with the harbour development proposals were made for the new settlement to be called Pulteneytown after Telford's patron. It was the only one of the society's villages to be completely designed by Telford and built, over a period of 20 years, on the lines which he laid down. Since Wick was an established royal burgh dating back to 1589 there was no need to provide civic buildings. The new settlement had to provide residential accommodation for the fisherfolk and buildings to house fish-

Previous page: Fig. 1 *Telford's Feu Plan, Lower Pulteneytown.*

processing activities. A bridge, designed by Telford, linked the new settlement on the south side of the river with the existing town of Wick on the north bank. Telford sited the main residential area on the elevated ground above the river terrace. The proposals followed, on a modest scale, the ideas of the period which influenced the layout of contemporary developments in Scottish cities and new settlements. The layout in its final form consisted of a hierarchy of streets set on a regular right-angled grid leading to an elegant rectangular space influenced in its form and landscaping by the squares of Edinburgh New Town or Bath (Sir William Pulteney was married to the heiress to the earldom of Bath). Telford divided the layout into 72 lots each 50ft (15.2m) on the street frontage and 100ft (30.5m) deep. Almost the whole frontage was to be filled and the buildings were to be right on the street. Front gardens were not permitted as it was thought that these encouraged the development of middens on the main streets.

There was ample garden ground behind as Pulteneytown, unlike the society's western villages, was not intended for crofter fishermen. It was for professional fishermen who could earn enough to pay for any food which they did not grow in their back gardens or take from the sea. Each house had access to its back garden via a pend.

Telford suggested plans for each house and specified storey heights, proportions of openings and construction of pavements and roadways. He hoped for 'uniformity of Building in point of Elevation of the Houses and Dimensions of Doors and Windows'. The main streets were to have two-storey houses while the lesser streets could be single storey. All houses were to be stone-built with slate roofs. Since the lots were allocated to individual owners and builders, Telford's intentions were not fully realised. In 1815 he admitted that the houses were not built to specification and hardly two were alike but agreed that to challenge them would lead to endless disputes.

Lower Pulteneytown was the working area of the town consisting of accommodation for activities associated with the herring fishing industry. These included gutting, curing, coopering and packing. The area of sandy links adjacent to the harbour was divided into 21 lots for curing houses each 60ft (18.3m) x 120ft (36.6m). The curing houses were to be at least 60ft (18.3m) x 22ft (6.7m) x 18ft (5.5m) high with sheds and cellars at the rear. The frontage, which had to be filled, could be used for a dwelling house provided it was 18ft (5.5m) high and the sheds built at the side of the lot. The buildings had to be used by fish curers, fishermen or people employed by them.

Fig. 1 *Model of Pulteneytown.* Photograph Shelley Tavendale

The layout of Lower Pulteneytown was less architecturally ambitious than the upper part of the town. The streets form a regular grid set at right angles to the harbour quay modified on the south side by the angle of the steep slope which separates the area from Upper Pulteneytown. There is no hierarchy of streets or spaces. The buildings are built to the back of the pavements enclosing the courts in which the work took place. Access to the courtyards is by means of pends wide enough to admit carts and surmounted by the characteristic flat arches often attributed to Telford, although it is doubtful if he was involved in their design.

Pulteneytown proved to be a highly successful venture and by the mid-19th century Wick was a leading herring fishing port. The number of fishing boats using the harbour rose from 200 in 1795 to over 1000 in the 1820s. In the 1840s the six weeks for the herring fishing season in July and August saw an influx of some 10,000 immigrant workers to the town (the resident population at the time was approximately 6000). The incoming workers were accommodated in crowded conditions in the lofts above the curing houses in Lower Pulteneytown. Some indication of their lifestyle can be found in the descriptions of the Rev. Charles Thomson who wrote in 1840:

'The herring fishing has increased wealth but also wickedness. No care is taken of the 10,000 young strangers of both sexes who are crowded together with the inhabitants within the narrow limits of Wick during the six weeks of the fishery, when they are exposed to drink and every other temptation ... Fever of a typhoid type is seldom absent and is acute during the fishing season. There is a great consumption of spirits, there being 22 public houses in Wick, and 23 in Pulteneytown ... Seminaries of Satan and Belial.'[1]

1. Edinburgh Central Library, *Statistical Account of Scotland, 1840,* Vol.XV, p. 17.

Despite Telford's efforts to contain fish processing within enclosed courtyards Thomson writes of the filth in the streets being indescribable: 'a putrescent effluvia steaming up from the fish offal'[2]. The great wealth resulting from the herring fishing allowed the more successful fish merchants to move from Pulteneytown to large villas in the suburbs which developed to the west of the town in the late Victorian period.

2. *op. cit.,* p. 17.

After the First World War the herring fishing declined and with it the prosperity of Pulteneytown. In the 1960s part of Upper Pulteneytown was demolished to make way for local authority housing. Fortunately Argyle Square, the centrepiece of Telford's layout, and the surrounding streets have survived to be protected by conservation area status. The buildings of Lower Pulteneytown fell into disuse and in 1992 the area was characterised by a mixture of large-scale modern industrial buildings, unsympathetic housing, vacant land and derelict buildings. The area is now being regenerated as part of the Wick Project under the auspices of Highland Regional Council.

Lower Pulteneytown with its strong grid of streets and courtyards provides an ideal introduction to early 19th century urban layout for students of architecture. The manner in which the clarity of the original concept has been eroded in the 20th century is also evident. These studies lead to the preparation of proposals to repair the damage caused by neglect and unsympathetic interventions to restore the urban form to accommodate future development which lays a foundation for the study of more complex, larger scale urban areas later in the course.

References:

J. Dunlop, *The British Fisheries Society 1786–1893,* 1978.

Scottish Records Office, *British Fisheries Society Papers.*

Scottish Records Office, *British Fisheries Society Minute Books 1808–1839.*

Edinburgh Central Library, *Statistical Account of Scotland 1840 vol. XV.*

The Authors

Bill Brogden is Reader in Architecture at the Scott Sutherland School of Architecture, The Robert Gordon University. Trained at North Carolina State University, he did his doctoral research at Edinburgh on *18th-Century Landscape Design*. A past chairman of the Architectural Heritage Society of Scotland, and a chairman of the North-East Group he is a council member of the National Trust for Scotland and the Garden History Society, Scottish Group. He is author of *Aberdeen an Illustrated Architectural Guide* and teaches urban architecture in the OUA at post-graduate level. A partner in the Castlegate Design Group he does a limited amount of architectural practice.

John Donald qualified in architecture at the Scott Sutherland School of Architecture in Aberdeen and graduated with an MSc in Rural and Regional Resource Planning at Aberdeen University. After a period of private practice in Edinburgh he joined the staff of Scott Sutherland School of Architecture, where he is currently Deputy Head. He has combined teaching with practice in partnership with his wife, Marion, and is Cases Convenor of the North-East Group of the Architectural Heritage Society of Scotland. In 1992-3 he led a student project on the history and future development of Lower Pulteneytown, Wick, which was commissioned by Highland Regional Council as part of their programme for the regeneration of the area.

Brian M. Evans is a chartered town planner, chartered designer and partner of Gillespies, the multi-disciplinary design practice. Following his role in the masterplanning and design coordination of the Glasgow Garden Festival 1988, he has contributed to the urban regeneration programme in Glasgow and carried out urban design projects in many towns and cities throughout Scotland and in England, Ireland and Europe. He contributes to the urban design programmes of the Scott Sutherland School of Architecture, Aberdeen, and the School of Housing and Planning at Edinburgh College of Art.

Miles Glendinning works at RCAHMS and is an honorary fellow at the Department of Social Policy, University of Edinburgh. He is author (with Stefan Muthesius) of *Tower Block: Modern Housing in England, Scotland, Wales and Northern Ireland*, 1994 and (with Ranald MacInnes and Aonghus Mackechnie) of *A History of Scottish Architecture from the Renaissance to the Present Day* (forthcoming).

Neil Lamb is a Chartered Architect who trained and teaches architecture at the Scott Sutherland School of Architecture. Having practised with Arup Associates in London he is presently working on his doctoral thesis on the *Teaching of Architectural Theory*. He teaches post-graduate students urban architecture in the OUA and conducts a limited amount of architectural practice.

John Lowrey is Lecturer in architectural history at Edinburgh University. His research is in late 17th- and early 18th-century Scottish garden and landscape design. He is editor of the Architectural Heritage Society of Scotland's Journal *Architectural Heritage*.

Professor **Charles McKean** is Head of the School of Architecture at Duncan of Jordanstone College, University of Dundee. For 15 years secretary and treasurer of the Royal Incorporation of Architects in Scotland, he is a well-respected journalist and author of several publications, notably titles in the RIAS/Landmark Trust series of illustrated architectural guides to Scotland. He is an honorary member of the Saltire Society, a member of the council of the Architectural Heritage Society of Scotland, a member of the Architecture Club and the Scottish Museums Council.

Patrick Nuttgens was born in 1930, was educated at Radcliffe College, Edinburgh College of Art and Edinburgh University, where he graduated in 1954. After doctoral research on *Planned Villages of the North-East of Scotland* he taught at Edinburgh University. In 1970 he became the first director of Leeds Polytechnic. Disabled as a result from multiple sclerosis, he retired from the polytechnic in 1986 and was appointed Honorary Professor of the University of York. He is author of many books on architecture and planning, including *The Landscape of Ideas*, 1972 and *The Story of Architecture*, 1983. He is President of York Georgian Society and the chairman of York Theatre Royal.

Peter Reed is Professor of Architecture at the University of Strathclyde, Glasgow. He is editor of *Glasgow: The Forming of a City, Edinburgh*, 1993, and he established the Association of Scottish Schools of Architecture and acted for many years as its secretary.

Gavin Stamp is Lecturer in architectural history at the Mackintosh School of Architecture in Glasgow. He appears frequently and authoritatively in the press and on television. He has founded the Thirties Society (now the 20th-Century Society) and the Alexander Thomson Society.

Frank Arneil Walker is Professor of Architecture at the University of Strathclyde, Glasgow. He has written several architectural guides and has contributed to numerous books on architectural and urban history including *Charles Rennie Mackintosh: The Architectural Papers* and *Glasgow: The Forming of a City*.